# *Easy* Reversible Vests

## Carol Doak

That Patchwork Place®

## Dedication

To Sherry Reis for a special friendship that has enriched my life beyond measure.

## Acknowledgments

My heartfelt thanks and appreciation are extended to:
My students in the Reversible Vest classes for their infectious enthusiasm;
Carol Boer, Roxanne Carter, Moira Clegg, Ginny Guaraldi, Beckie Hansen, Pam Ludwig, and Terry Maddox for sharing their reversible vests.
My husband, Alan, for his constant support and encouragement for all my endeavors;
Barbara Weiland and Ursula Reikes for their vision, delightful support, and friendship.

## Credits

Editor-in-Chief . . . . . . . . . . Barbara Weiland
Technical Editors . . . . . . . . . . Ursula Reikes
                                      Sharon Rose
Managing Editor . . . . . . . . . . . . Greg Sharp
Copy Editor . . . . . . . . . . . . . . Liz McGehee
Proofreaders . . . . . . . . . . . . . . . Tina Cook
                                      Leslie Phillips
Illustrator . . . . . . . . . . . . . . . Laurel Strand
Illustration Assistant . . . . . . . Lisa McKenney
Photographer . . . . . . . . . . . . . . Brent Kane
Design Director . . . . . . . . . . . . . Judy Petry
Text and Cover Designer . . . . . . Kay Green
Design Assistant . . . . . . . . . . . Shean Bemis

Easy Reversible Vests
©1995 by Carol Doak

That Patchwork Place, Inc., PO Box 118, Bothell, WA 98041-0118 USA

Printed in the United States of America
00 99 98 97 96 95 6 5 4 3

### MISSION STATEMENT

WE ARE DEDICATED TO PROVIDING QUALITY PRODUCTS THAT ENCOURAGE CREATIVITY AND PROMOTE SELF-ESTEEM IN OUR CUSTOMERS AND OUR EMPLOYEES.

WE STRIVE TO MAKE A DIFFERENCE IN THE LIVES WE TOUCH.

*That Patchwork Place is an employee-owned, financially secure company.*

**Library of Congress Cataloging-in-Publication Data**
Doak, Carol.
    Easy reversible vests / Carol Doak.
       p.   cm.
    ISBN 1-56477-092-3
    1. Vests.  I. Title.
TT615.D63 1995
646.4'5—dc20                    94-42066
                                      CIP

# Contents

Preface                                          4

Introduction                                     4

Vest Styles                                      5

Fabric & Color Selection                         6
  Main-Player Fabrics . . . . . . . . . . . . . . . . . 6
  Supporting Fabrics . . . . . . . . . . . . . . . . . 7
  Accent Fabrics . . . . . . . . . . . . . . . . . . . 9
  Choosing Fabric for Reversible Vests  . . . 9

Piecing Techniques                              10
  Fabric Preparation . . . . . . . . . . . . . . . . . 10
    Cutting the Foundation  . . . . . . . . . . 10
    Cutting One-Piece Sections . . . . . . . 10
  Technique One— Adding Strips
    to a Foundation . . . . . . . . . . . . . . . . 11
  Technique Two— Sewing Squares
    to Create a New Fabric . . . . . . . . . . 20
  Technique Three—Combining Strips, Squares,
    and Blocks on a Foundation  . . . . . . 26

Embellishments                                  30
  Prairie Points . . . . . . . . . . . . . . . . . . . . 30
  Decorative Topstitching  . . . . . . . . . . . 31
  Fabric Manipulations . . . . . . . . . . . . . . 31
  Ribbons and Lace  . . . . . . . . . . . . . . . . 31
  Trinkets, Baubles, and Beads . . . . . . . . 31
  Shoulder Accents . . . . . . . . . . . . . . . . . 32

Reversible Vests                                33
  Two Vests for the Price of One . . . . . . . 33

Gallery of Vests                                34

Vests for Inspiration                           40

Vest Patterns                                   49
  Red Hot Strippers  . . . . . . . . . . . . . . . 50
  Blue, Blue Waves  . . . . . . . . . . . . . . . 51
  Oriental Tea Garden . . . . . . . . . . . . . 52
  Sunny Spring . . . . . . . . . . . . . . . . . . . 53
  Springtime Tulips  . . . . . . . . . . . . . . . 54
  Emeralds and Sapphires . . . . . . . . . . 55
  Blue Birds of Paradise  . . . . . . . . . . . . 56
  Fancy Turquoise  . . . . . . . . . . . . . . . . 58
  Something Old  . . . . . . . . . . . . . . . . . 60
  Madam Butterfly . . . . . . . . . . . . . . . . 62
  Something Blue  . . . . . . . . . . . . . . . . . 65
  Blue and Purple Passions  . . . . . . . . . . 66
  Morning Glory . . . . . . . . . . . . . . . . . . 67
  Hearts and Flowers  . . . . . . . . . . . . . . 68

Assembly and Finishing                          70
  Elastic  . . . . . . . . . . . . . . . . . . . . . . . . 71
  Side Seams  . . . . . . . . . . . . . . . . . . . . 71
  Vest Style C—Side Vent Option  . . . . . . 72
  Buttons and Closures . . . . . . . . . . . . . . 72

Block Designs                                   74
  Paper-Pieced Block Designs . . . . . . . . 74

Resource List                                   88

About the Author                                88

# Preface

**W**hat began for me as a solution to a wardrobe dilemma has become a full-scale passion. My dilemma was what to do with various shades of red clothing that just didn't seem to go well together. My solution was to make a vest from a group of fabrics, each of which matched a piece of clothing. The vest acted as a bridge between the various shades. I relied upon quick and easy construction techniques that offered many design options and almost instant gratification. This vest led to another vest, and so the passion began.

Since being able to make the vests quickly and easily was a priority, I often used large-scale print fabrics for one vest front to create interest without effort. These large-scale prints also offered a source of color combinations for the accompanying pieced front. The initial vests were quick, machine-pieced strips sewn to a fabric foundation. Incorporating another of my patchwork passions, paper-pieced quilt blocks, seemed like a natural next step. These intricate designs that work up so quickly and easily offered focus and detail for more vest designs. They could be pieced with fabric squares to create a new fabric from which the vest fronts could be cut. I also used paper-pieced blocks in conjunction with strips sewn to a foundation for many more design possibilities. These easy patchwork techniques offered a great deal of flexibility and design options. Decorative machine stitching and other easy fabric embellishments added pizzazz without a lot of extra trouble.

Although I constructed the vests so they could be reversible, it was my friend Sherry Reis who first suggested I make the lining into a whole separate vest by piecing it differently and using different fabrics. This option yielded two fashion statements for the price of one!

Each time I wore a reversible vest, people would comment about the striking combination of fabrics and details. It wasn't long before I was teaching others how they too could make reversible vests using these easy techniques. What I wasn't prepared for was the way these methods permitted the unique personalities of their makers to shine through. It was so much fun to see how individuals used the same techniques to create strikingly different vests. Even the same person could create a carefree casual side and an elegant dressy side in the same vest. The possibilities seemed endless. I wrote *Easy Reversible Vests* in order to share these easy techniques and this passion.

# Introduction

**E**asy Reversible Vests shares my techniques for quick and easy vests with an overall subtle quality. Many of these vests are "make today and wear tomorrow" projects! With only four seams, the vest patterns are very simple to construct, yet the styles are figure flattering. Since fabric selection plays such an important role in these vests, the Fabric and Color Selection section covers methods for grouping fabrics and selecting "main-player" fabrics to set the themes for your vests. The "Piecing Techniques" section describes the quick and easy construction methods and some of the many design options they offer. Options for creating special detail in your vest are described in the "Embellishment" section, and a variety of paper-pieced block designs are presented in the "Paper-Pieced Block Design" section. The "Gallery of Vests" and "Vests for Inspiration" include photographs of a variety of vests that demonstrate some of the infinite design and fabric possibilities. The "Assembly and Finishing" section tells you how to put together a reversible vest.

You will read the words "you can" often, because I seek to inspire you to consider the many options available as you easily create one-of-a-kind reversible fashion vests that fit your personality, style, and wardrobe.

**F**ull-scale patterns for the following vest styles are provided on the pullout pattern sheets.

**Vest Style A:** This vest style has high, straight fronts coming to a central point. The straight fronts provide a larger area for patchwork. The back of the vest also has a central point at the lower hem. The vest is slightly shorter than Vest Style B.

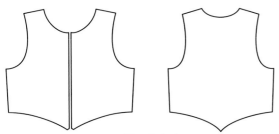

Vest Style A

**Vest Style B:** This is a loose-fitting waistcoat style vest with a straight back hem and two front hem points.

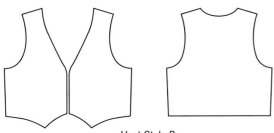

Vest Style B

**Vest Style B Option:** This style is similar to Vest Style B except that the back hem is double-pointed, mimicking the front.

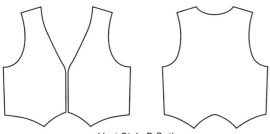

Vest Style B Option

**Vest Style C:** This is a longer vest style with optional side vents. The longer lines are more flattering on some figures. The shoulders are wider and the bottom hems are curved.

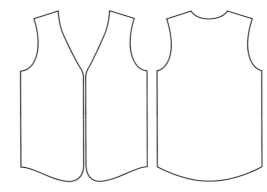

Vest Style C

Make a tracing-paper copy of the vest pattern pieces in the style and size of your choice. Copying the pattern allows you to keep all the vest pattern sizes and styles intact. Because it is transparent, tracing paper also makes it easier to place certain design elements where you want them. Mark the right sides of the left and right vest fronts on your copies with a red pencil. This will alert you when you are cutting fabric for the vest fronts so you won't become confused!

These vest patterns include a ⅜"-wide seam allowance (less bulky than the usual ⅝"). You can also use an appropriate commercial vest pattern if you prefer. Purchased vest patterns should consist of one back pattern piece and one front pattern piece. Do not use patterns that contain darts, slip pockets, or other piecing requirements, such as fitted bodices. If the commercial pattern has a ⅝"-wide seam allowance, simply stitch as directed and trim the seam allowances to ⅜".

**It is important to check that the size and style you have selected will provide a good fit before you begin creating your vest. Cut out muslin pattern pieces and baste them at the shoulder and side seams to check the fit. Adjust these seams as necessary for a better fit. You don't want to go to the trouble of making your patchwork vest only to find out later that it doesn't fit as you would like.**

Note: If you want to make a vest that does not button, cut the front pattern pieces ⅜" from the Center Front line, to allow for seam allowances.

# Fabric & Color Selection

 onsider the task of putting together a group of fabrics for your vest similar to the task of putting together a major-league baseball team. First you select your pitcher, or "main-player fabric."

A good pitcher is out on the field for several innings and gets everyone's attention. Similarly, a main-player fabric should be a striking, beautiful print. Use it for one whole vest front or several times in the patchwork. Not every baseball team has a really good pitcher that stands out. You can make your vest without a main-player fabric, but it's easiest to start with one and base your other fabric selections on it.

A pitcher needs a team of outfielders and infielders to work as a group and support him. Your supporting "team" should include four to eight different fabrics that blend well with each other and work with your main-player fabric.

Lastly, your team needs a star home-run hitter. He is only noticed when he comes to bat, but he gets lots of attention. The stars of your vest are accent fabrics that are used sparingly. Put it all together and you are on your way to winning the World Series!

Fabric and color play an important role in the look of the vest and offer a wide variety of style options. If you are a quiltmaker, you probably have a selection of cotton fabrics on hand that can be incorporated into your vests. If you select one of the foundation-piecing techniques, you can also easily include fabrics that are not normally used in patchwork, such as satins, lamés, moirés, knits, metallics, silks, and other specialty fabrics. Since many of the vests rely upon small pieces for strips, squares, and paper-pieced patchwork blocks, you can use even the smallest piece of specialty fabric.

When deciding which colors to use, keep your wardrobe in mind. Base your fabric selections on hard-to-match clothing, and whatever you do, choose colors that flatter you or that you feel comfortable wearing. If you have had your colors "done" and have a swatch book, refer to it as you select fabrics for your vest.

## Main-Player Fabrics— "The Pitcher"

I use the term "main-player fabric" because large- and medium-scale print fabrics can make a dramatic statement and play an important part in the look of the vest. Use the main-player fabric to set the theme and style of your vest and to inspire your other fabric choices.

For the person who finds it difficult to put a group of fabrics together for patchwork, this is a great place to start. If you choose a print because you like it, you already know you like that particular mix of colors. You can confidently proceed to choose the remainder of the fabrics for the patchwork from the colors in the main-player fabric. The background color of the main-player fabric can be the source for the supporting fabrics in the patchwork and a small-scale print fabric for the back. For a striking look, the metallic highlights in main-player fabrics that contain gold or silver can be carried through on the patchwork side of the vest with lamé or knitted metallic fabrics in thin strips or tiny bits of patchwork. See the photographs on pages 43 and 44 for examples of vests inspired by striking main-player fabrics.

### Large-Scale Prints

Large-scale florals and paisleys make good main-player fabrics. Choose fabrics with colors that blend rather than contrast—a large-scale graphic design, such as a stark black-and-white floral might make too much of a statement.

Japanese fabrics, such as Yukata, are large-scale main-player fabrics that work wonderfully for one vest front. They often have a hand-painted look with soft design elements such as large-scale flowers and butterflies. Featuring them on one vest front with patchwork on the other provides interesting detail without effort. Their large, curved lines soften the angles in the patchwork. They are only about 15" wide, but you can join them to other fabrics to cover the pattern piece if necessary. (See Tip on page 57.)

## Medium-Scale Multicolor Prints

A medium-scale print of several colors is another main-player option. These prints can again serve as the inspiration for the other fabrics in the vest and can act as the bridge between several colors for a more coordinated look in the patchwork.

# Supporting Fabrics— "The Outfielders"

When selecting fabrics to go with your main-player fabric, keep in mind that you want a subtle overall look. Value is the darkness or lightness of a color and should be considered when looking at colors within fabrics as well as between fabrics. Avoid strong value contrasts between your supporting fabrics because the vest will look too busy.

## Value within Fabrics

You can achieve a subtle look by using fabrics with similar values and/or colors within. A print fabric that contains several colors should have only slight contrast in value. Avoid print fabrics with too high a contrast in value; they are distracting and do not blend well. Tone-on-tone fabrics work well as supporting fabrics.

*These prints have similar values and blend well as a group.*

*These prints have a high contrast in value and do not blend well as a group.*

## Value between Fabrics

Combining fabrics in several different colors of similar value can present a subtle look with a bit of interest. For example, a group of pastels or light-colored prints will have a subtle look. Use a Ruby Beholder™ to determine the relative values of a group of fabrics. The tinted plastic eliminates color and reveals only the value of each color.

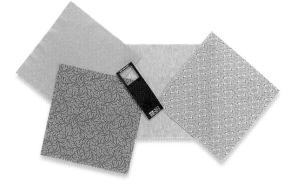

Vests combining several deep, dark colors, such as black, navy, forest green, and burgundy are another good example. A background of deep, dark colors showcases paper-pieced patchwork blocks nicely. Since there is very little contrast between dark colors, the fabrics create a subtle basis for the patchwork.

## Fabrics of the Same Color

Another option is to select a group of fabrics that are various shades of the same color in varying print scales and a slightly wider range of values. This type of fabric grouping will appear as one color, with a little bit of interest provided by the varying print scales and shades. One-color fabric groupings are wonderful bridges that allow you to wear slightly different shades of that color clothing. I have found this method of fabric selection particularly helpful with the reds and greens in my wardrobe.

Neutrals, such as blacks, grays, and beiges, make wonderful supporting fabrics. They are easy to blend, do not call attention to themselves, and can support completely different main-player or accent colors on the two sides of a reversible vest. You can use black fabrics with red and green on one side of the vest and with blue and pink on the reverse side. Use one of the neutral fabrics for shoulder accents or button loops that will show on both sides.

## Accent Fabrics— "The Home-Run Hitters"

Use color, value, texture, or glitter to add the accent, the spark, the pinch of salt in the soup. Remember, an accent is just that—use it sparingly. A pinch of salt enhances the flavor, but a quarter cup spoils the soup.

- Contrasting color creates an accent. A vest in various shades of green benefits from the addition of a pink or burgundy accent.
- A vest of medium-value fabrics benefits from the addition of one really dark fabric.
- Texture, such as the shine of a satin, the subtle lines of a moiré, or the smooth look of a polished cotton, catches the eye of the viewer and adds interest.
- And finally, fabrics that have a little metallic gold or silver in them add real sparkle. If you use one of the foundation-piecing methods, bits of lamé and metallic knit fabrics can be included for a dressy look.

## A Special Note on Fabrics for Paper-Pieced Patchwork Blocks

If you decide to use paper-pieced patchwork blocks in your vest, you want them to stand out from the surrounding patchwork. For this, you need contrast. An easy way to do this is to select the lightest or darkest of your supporting fabrics and audition it for the background of the paper-pieced block. Does it stand out against the other fabrics in the group? If it does not, use an even lighter or darker fabric to get the contrast you need. For a different look, use one of your blending fabrics for the background and use only contrasting fabrics for the central paper-pieced motif. (See the Springtime Tulips vest on page 39.)

## Choosing Fabric for Reversible Vests

No matter how careful you are, the inside of a reversible vest might occasionally be visible around the outside edges. Very dark or bright fabrics can also show through if the fabrics on the other side are light. For this reason, it is best to choose somewhat similar fabrics in value for the two sides. One way to do this is to use a neutral color, such as gray or black, with two completely different color schemes on the two sides. One side might be pink and blue with black, and the other side might be red and green with black.

Other than that, the possibilities are endless! One side of the vest might have satins and gold fabrics for a dressy look, and the other side calicoes and small prints for a more casual look. This can be a real bonus for the traveler who likes to pack light—one piece of clothing works with jeans during the day and dresses up a plain dress for evening wear.

## Tools and Supplies

Listed below are some of the tools and supplies you will need to make your reversible vest.

### The Basics

Sewing machine in good working order with a walking foot for foundation piecing and vest assembly

Sewing-machine needles, size 90/14 for paper piecing and size 80/12 for general sewing

Rotary cutter and mat

3½" x 24" rotary-cutting ruler

6" or 8" Bias Square®

Tracing paper for the paper-pieced blocks and vest patterns

Pressing cloth to protect delicate fabrics

Lightweight fusible interfacing

### Optional Extras

Ruby Beholder™

Sewing-machine topstitch needles for machine embroidery

Decorative machine-embroidery thread

Hera® Fabric Marker*

Miniturn™ tool for turning bias strips right side out to make button loops*

Stuff-It II™ tool for pushing out points and edges of the vest after it is turned right side out*

Easy Machine Paper Piecing by Carol Doak (That Patchwork Place, Inc.)

*See the Resource List on page 88.

# Piecing Techniques

## Fabric Preparation

Prewash all washable fabrics. Press laundered fabrics to remove any wrinkles. Do not prewash specialty fabrics, such as velvets, silks, and satins. These are generally dry-cleaned. Use a woven 100% cotton fusible interfacing to stabilize delicate fabrics, such as lamés and lightweight silks.

## Cutting the Foundation

Use 100% cotton for your foundation fabric. If most of your fabrics are dark, use a dark solid. If the fabrics are mostly light, use a light-colored fabric, such as muslin.

To make the foundation, pin the pattern piece to the fabric and cut around the perimeter. To cut out two identically shaped front foundations, fold the fabric and cut both pieces at once.

To cut out back foundation, fold fabric and place center back on fold.

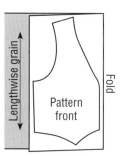

Cut pattern front from double layer for 2 pattern fronts.

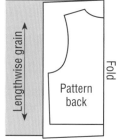

Place pattern back on fold.

**Important:** Mark the two front foundation pieces "left" and "right" so you don't sew two left sides or two right sides by mistake. Even if you only make one front foundation, mark the right side of the fabric so you don't end up sewing strips to the wrong side.

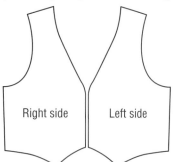

Right side    Left side

## Cutting One-Piece Sections

If you are using one piece of fabric for a vest front or back, cut these pieces out now so you will have the remaining fabric available for patchwork. (See page 49 for more about one-piece sections.)

The chart below indicates the yardage needed for one-piece sections or multiple one-piece sections from the same vest fabric or foundation fabric in the three vest styles. For example: If you are making a size small Vest Style A, a ¾-yard piece (either foundation fabric or a vest fabric) is wide enough to cut one front, or one back, or two fronts, or one front and one back, or two fronts and one back. However, if you are making a medium Vest Style A, you will need 1½ yards to cut two fronts and one back from the same piece of fabric.

### Yardage Requirements for Whole Pattern Pieces (44"-wide fabrics)

| Vest Styles A and B and B Option | | | | |
|---|---|---|---|---|
| 1 Front* | 1 Back | 2 Fronts | 1 Front and 1 Back | 2 Fronts and 1 Back |
| **P** ¾ yd | ¾ yd | ¾ yd | ¾ yd | ¾ yd |
| **S** ¾ yd | ¾ yd | ¾ yd | ¾ yd | ¾ yd |
| **M** ¾ yd | ¾ yd | ¾ yd | ¾ yd | 1½ yds |
| **L** ¾ yd | ¾ yd | ¾ yd | ¾ yd | 1½ yds |
| **XL** ¾ yd | ¾ yd | ¾ yd | ¾ yd | 1½ yds |
| **Vest Style C** | | | | |
| **P** 1 yd | 1 yd | 1 yd | 1 yd | 2 yds |
| **S** 1 yd | 1 yd | 1 yd | 1 yd | 2 yds |
| **M** 1 yd | 1 yd | 1 yd | 1 yd | 2 yds |
| **L** 1 yd | 1 yd | 1 yd | 1 yd | 2 yds |
| **XL** 1 yd** | 1 yd | 1 yd | 2 yds | 2 yds |

*"Front" refers to either a right or left front pattern piece.
**The 15"-wide Yukata fabric is wide enough to cut one front pattern piece for all sizes and vest styles EXCEPT for Vest Style C, size XL. A fabric strip can be added to either the center front or the side to accommodate the pattern piece.

# Technique One— Adding Strips to a Foundation

Sewing strips of fabric to a fabric foundation is a quick and easy way to create patchwork vests. Use this method to create patchwork on all or just some of the vest pattern pieces.

## Cutting Strips

*To cut fabric strips for foundation piecing:*

1. Fold the fabric in half with the selvages matching.
2. Position the fabric on the cutting mat with the fold closest to you and the uneven edges on your left. (Reverse these directions if you are left-handed.)
3. Line up one edge of an 8" square ruler even with the fold of the fabric. Position a long ruler to the left of the square and remove the square.

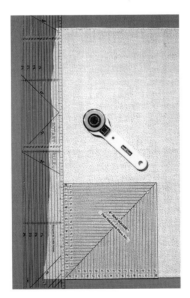

4. Use a rotary cutter and cut along the right-hand edge of the ruler to make a clean cut across the width of the fabric. Cut away from yourself, using firm, downward pressure. Be careful not to let the ruler slip out of position as you cut. Discard the trimmed edge.

5. Cut strips of fabric, aligning the clean cut edge of the fabric with the ruler markings at the desired width.

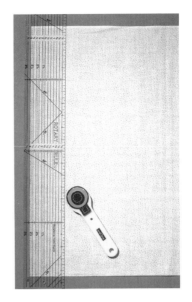

Note: Strips can be all the same width or of varying widths. I usually cut strips that range from 1" to 2½" wide. A design worked in 1" finished strips looks quite different when worked in 2" finished strips. To gain perspective on the finished size of the strips you intend to cut, place the rotary ruler on the fabric at the finished size. When you decide on a finished size, simply add ½" for the seam allowances to determine the cut size.

## Placing Strips

You can place strips on the vest foundation vertically, horizontally, or diagonally.

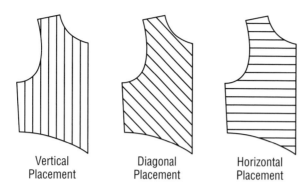

Vertical Placement    Diagonal Placement    Horizontal Placement

Some designs are more figure flattering than others. Vests with strips placed diagonally toward the center front are generally more flattering than those with strips placed diagonally out toward the hips. Vertically placed strips in the lower portion of the vest are much more flattering than horizontally placed strips. Experiment a little to see what works best for you.

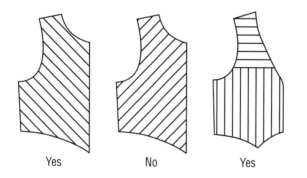

Yes    No    Yes

You can also change directions by piecing strips in one direction first and then adding strips in another direction. (See page 19 for instructions to add strips in two directions.)

Sew these strips first and sew the first opposite-direction strip across raw edges.

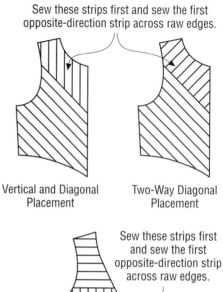

Vertical and Diagonal Placement    Two-Way Diagonal Placement

Sew these strips first and sew the first opposite-direction strip across raw edges.

Two-Way Horizontal and Vertical Placement

In addition to placing the strips in different directions to create interest and flatter the figure, you can use strip width, color, and value as design elements. Strip widths can be all the same, alternate, form a repetitive pattern, or vary randomly.

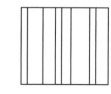

Strips all same width    Alternating strip widths

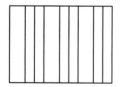

Strip widths that create pattern    Strip widths that vary randomly

Colors can be placed in a consistent fashion, alternate, form a pattern, or vary randomly. Only one strip width is used in this example; remember that widths can also vary as discussed previously.

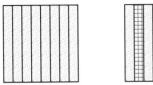
Strips all same color

Alternating colors

Colors that form
a pattern

Random colors

You can also deliberately place strips of certain values for an effect. Again for the sake of example, strips of the same width are depicted; widths can vary.

Strips of same value

Alternating value

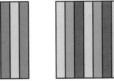
Patterned value

Random value

Values that range
from dark to light

For an organized individual, the tendency to repeat a sequence comes naturally. Random placement of fabric widths, colors, and values is sometimes difficult. To force myself to be random, I sometimes pick up the next strip without looking and only switch if it is identical to the strip that preceded it.

## Adding Pieced Segments

You can add interest to whole-fabric strips by inserting small pieced segments of patchwork. To break up full-length strips with segments of patchwork:

1. Cut short strips, all the same length, from four or five of your cut strips.
2. Sew the strips together as shown below, using a 1/4"-wide seam allowance.
3. Press the seam allowances in one direction.
4. Place the strip unit on the cutting mat and trim one short edge cleanly. Cut segments in the same width or widths as the full-length strips you are using.

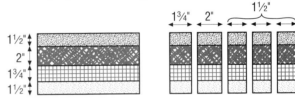

5. Sew these pieced segments randomly to the whole-fabric strips at the beginning, end, or in the middle, then add the pieced strips to the foundation.

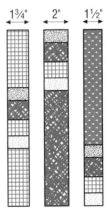

## Adding Pieced Strips

You can also alternate full-length strips of fabric with pieced strips cut vertically or diagonally. Place the pieced units with the fabrics in the same position each time for a continuous look, or offset fabrics from strip to strip. Offsetting yields different results, depending on whether fabrics in the pieced strips are all of the same width or not. Pieced sections may also be placed in a random fashion. Although the illustration shows these options using straight-cut strips placed vertically, you can do the same with horizontal and diagonal placements and diagonally cut pieced strips.

You can achieve another look by placing pieced strips and fabric strips diagonally on the foundation.

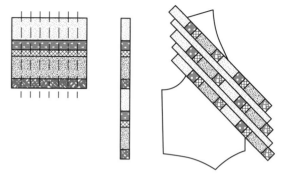

**Same-Size Pieced Strips**

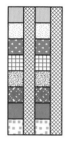

Fabric and seams are aligned.

Pieced strips are offset by one fabric.

Seams are randomly placed.

**Different-Width Pieced Strips**

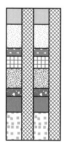

Fabric and seams are aligned.

Pieced strips are offset by one fabric.

## Making Pieced Strips

*To make straight-cut pieced strips:*

1. Join several fabric strips of the same width or varying widths along the long edges.
2. Crosscut the strips at the same width and join the segments end to end until the unit is long enough to cover the foundation.

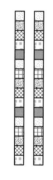

Note: If you want the pieced unit to form squares on the vest, use strips of uniform width to make the strip unit, then crosscut at the same width the original strips were cut. For example, if you joined 2" strips to make the strip unit, crosscut at 2" intervals.

3. Fabrics in the pieced strips can be aligned, offset, or random. After you sew a pieced strip to the foundation, trim even with the foundation edge and use the remainder as needed for subsequent rows.

*To make diagonally cut pieced strips:*
1. Join several strips of fabric of the same width or varying widths along the long edges.
2. Align the 45° line on your rotary ruler with one horizontal line of the strip unit. Make the first cut diagonally across the width of the strip unit. Align the desired width on the ruler with the diagonal cut edge of the fabric and keep the 45° line along a horizontal line of the strip unit. Continue to cut subsequent segments parallel to the first cut, in the desired width by moving the ruler down the pieced strip.

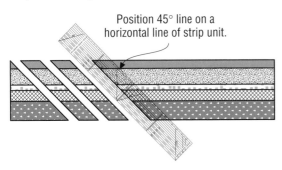

Position 45° line on a horizontal line of strip unit.

Note: Some rotary rulers show a 45° line going in both directions. Others have only one 45° line. You may need to turn the ruler over in order to place the 45° line on a horizontal seam line.

3. Join segments to create pieced strips long enough for diagonal placement on your vest.

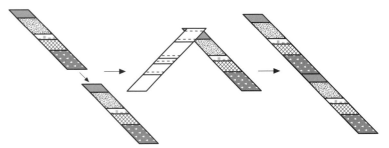

If the pieced strips are placed diagonally on the foundation in the same direction as they were cut, the seams will be horizontal. Fabrics in the pieced strips can be aligned, offset, or random.

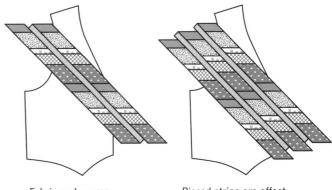

Fabric and seams are aligned.

Pieced strips are offset by one fabric.

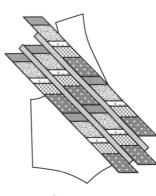

Seams are randomly placed.

If the pieced strips are placed diagonally on the foundation in the opposite direction from how they were cut, the seams will be vertical. Again, the pieced seams can be aligned, offset, or random.

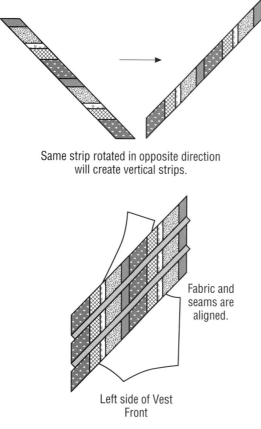

Same strip rotated in opposite direction will create vertical strips.

Fabric and seams are aligned.

Left side of Vest Front

If you plan to piece both vest fronts in a mirror-image manner, you will need to cut the pieced strips diagonally in one direction for one side and in the opposite direction for the other side. To cut strips in the opposite direction from those previously illustrated, simply place the ruler diagonally in the opposite direction and cut in the same way.

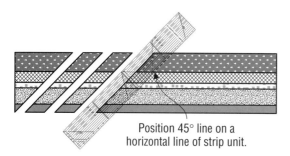

Position 45° line on a horizontal line of strip unit.

## TIP

Just so you don't become confused, the rule is that diagonally pieced strips placed in the same direction that they are cut appear horizontal. Pieced strips placed in the opposite direction from which they are cut appear vertical.

When you place diagonally cut pieced strips on the foundation vertically, still other design possibilities develop. The same options for aligning or offsetting the fabrics exist. Here again, if you want the pieced strips on the right and left fronts to mirror each other, cut them in opposite directions.

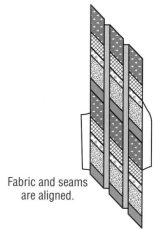

Fabric and seams are aligned.

## Sewing Strips on the Foundation

An even-feed or walking foot attachment on your sewing machine will help you sew smoothly through many layers. These attachments feed top and bottom fabrics through the machine at the same rate so the foundation remains flat. Let the sewing machine take the fabric—just steer the fabric strips into the needle. Don't tug on the fabric at all, as this can cause gathers or puckers.

1. Pin the first strip right side up in the center of the foundation, running either straight up and down, or at the desired angle.

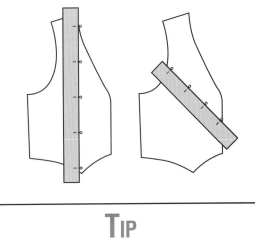

## TIP

To make sure the first strip is truly vertical, place a long see-through ruler along the front edge of the foundation and align the strip with the straight edge of the ruler.

2. Check the length of the second strip by placing it right side up on the foundation alongside the center strip. Remember that ¼" along each strip will be taken up by seam allowances. It is especially important to check the length of strips you are sewing at an angle. You will be surprised at how much length is required.

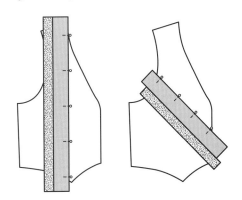

Length for next strip is determined with fabric right side up.

## TIP

The dangers of diagonal foundation piecing

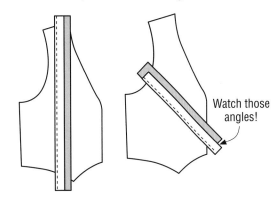

This strip looks long enough . . .

But see what happens when you open it out!

3. Place the second strip on the center strip with right sides together and raw edges even. Sew through both fabrics and the foundation, ¼" from the edge.

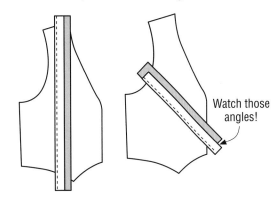

Watch those angles!

4. Open out the top strip and press with a dry iron on a cotton setting, or whatever setting is appropriate for the fabrics you are using.

Note: Let me add a special caution here about ironing any specialty fabrics (lamés, metallics, knits, silks, etc.) you may include in your pieced vest. Many of these specialty fabrics melt at higher heat settings, so be sure to use a pressing cloth and lower the heat setting.

5. Continue to add strips to the center strip, always checking length first, until half of the foundation is covered.

6. Return to the center and add strips to the other half of the foundation in the same manner. After all the strips have been added, trim the patchwork flush with the foundation fabric.

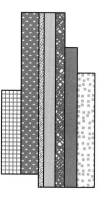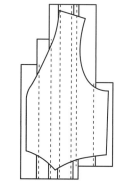

Vest front foundation with pieced strips as seen from right side.

Vest foundation as seen from back. Trim strips flush with foundation edge.

If you decide to align seams in successive or alternating straight-cut pieced strips, simply align the seams in each strip with the seams in the preceding pieced strip. Pin each seam in place.

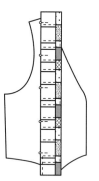

Aligning seams in diagonally cut pieced strips offers more of a challenge because the seams have to line up ¼" in from the edge, at the seam line.

1. Sew the first pieced strip and full-length fabric strip at the desired location.

2. Place the second pieced strip, right side up, alongside the full-length fabric strip, aligning seams of the two pieced strips approximately by eye.

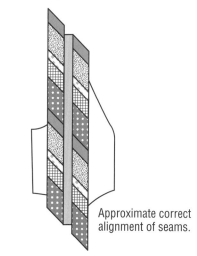

Approximate correct alignment of seams.

3. Carefully flip the second strip over so that right sides are together and pin in place ¼" from and parallel to the edge at the beginnning, end, and over a short distance in the middle. Open the strip and check for a good match. Adjust the position of the top strip until you achieve a good match.

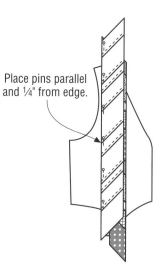

Place pins parallel and ¼" from edge.

4. Pin in place at each seam and check one last time before sewing.

*To add strips in two directions:*

1. Draw a pencil line on the foundation at the point where the edge of the first strip going in the other direction will be placed. This will be your "stop-sewing line." It includes a ¼"-wide seam allowance.

Stop-sewing line

2. Begin with the first group of strips and foundation-piece as usual. Stop sewing at the line.

3. When all the strips in the first group have been sewn, trim them as close to the line as possible.

4. Position the first strip going in the other direction on the sewn strips right side up. Always overestimate. It is better to cut away excess than to sew the strip and find it is too short. Turn the strip over so that right sides are together and raw edges are even; sew ¼" from edge.

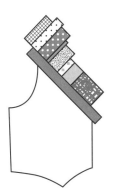
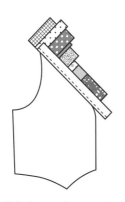

Position strip right side up to check for necessary length.

Note how end near center front extends to cover area once it is flipped.

5. Open the strip and press. Continue adding strips until the foundation is completely covered.

To make two matching vest fronts with two-directional piecing, place the foundations right sides together and mark the stop-sewing line with a Hera Fabric Marker. This will create an identical mirrored crease mark on both foundations.

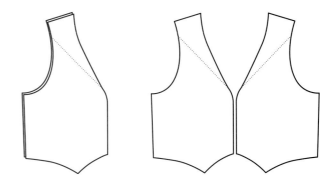

# Technique Two— Sewing Squares to Create a New Fabric

This technique involves sewing together squares of fabric, either whole or paper-pieced, to create a new piece of fabric from which the pattern pieces are cut. It does not use a foundation.

## Cutting Whole Squares

Cut squares from scraps or strips of fabric.

*To cut squares from scraps of fabric:*

1. Layer up to six scraps of fabric large enough to accommodate the size you need. Be sure to align the lengthwise and crosswise grains as much as possible.
2. Position the Bias Square on a corner of the fabric stack so that the edges are along the straight of grain.
3. Cut along two edges of the ruler.
4. Carefully turn the fabric layers around (or turn the mat) and position the Bias Square at the desired cutting size. Make the final two cuts to complete the fabric squares.

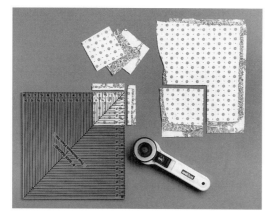

*To cut squares from a strip of fabric:*

1. Cut a strip the width of the cut size of the square. (See "Cutting Strips" on page 11.)
2. Turn the strip, line up the short end with the desired measurement on the Bias Square, and cut.

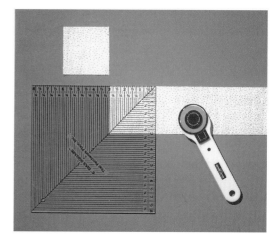

3. Continue in the same manner until the desired number of squares have been cut.

Note: You can layer several strips to save time.

## Making Paper-Pieced Blocks

Incorporating blocks made with quick and easy paper piecing techniques offers the delightful opportunity to include intricate patchwork blocks as focal points. Paper piecing also allows you to include specialty fabrics that are not usually used in patchwork, such as silks, satins, lamés, and metallic knits.

I have included several designs from my book *Easy Machine Paper Piecing* that I enjoy using on my vests, along with some new designs. The full-size patterns for these designs appear in the "Paper-Pieced Block Designs" section, beginning on page 75. The designs finish to 3" x 3". The Hearts and Flowers block is also offered in a 6" x 6" finished square. For more options, reduce any of the 4" x 4" paper-pieced designs in *Easy Machine Paper Piecing* to 3" x 3" on a copy machine: set the dial to 75% of the original.

If you plan to make Vest Style C or a purchased long vest pattern, you may want larger paper-pieced blocks. Make a paper pattern of the 3" design you would like to use. Place it on your vest in the desired location. Does it look small? Will it be swallowed up by the surrounding patchwork? If you need a bigger block, enlarge a design from this book or use a 4" block from *Easy Machine Paper Piecing*. To enlarge a 3" x 3" design to 4" x 4" on a copy machine, set the dial to 133%. Don't forget that all of the squares and/or strips you use with the larger block have to be larger as well. Another solution is to use more than one pieced block side by side to form a larger design.

## PREPARATION

1. Set the stitch length on the machine for approximately 18 to 20 stitches to the inch. A short stitch length perforates the paper better, so it is easier to tear away later. Use a 90/14 needle; the larger needle also helps perforate the paper.

2. Select a sewing thread that blends with most of the fabrics used.

3. Create a pressing and cutting area next to the machine by lowering the ironing board down to sewing level. Use one end to cut and the other end to press.

4. Have a small, sharp pair of scissors on hand to trim the fabric pieces after they are sewn.

5. Have your rotary cutter, 6" Bias Square ruler, and mat close at hand.

6. Set up a small lamp near the sewing machine. It is generally easy to place the first pieces without a light source, but a light is helpful for placing subsequent pieces of fabric when you need to be able to see through more layers.

7. Trace the block design onto tracing paper, transferring all seam lines and numbers. Cut the paper out 1/2" from the outside lines.

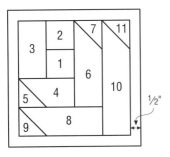

Trim paper pattern
1/2" from finish line.

Note: You can also use a copy machine to make duplicates of the design, but the copies must be made from the original drawing in this book (or *Easy Machine Paper Piecing*), as copy machines distort the image slightly. Do not make a copy from a copy; this compounds the distortion.

8. Select your fabric. The unmarked side of the block is the fabric side, which means the completed block is a mirror image of the drawn block design. To avoid any confusion, always note your fabric choices on the unmarked side of the block design.

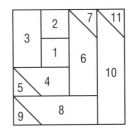 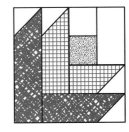

Paper-pieced design     Design as seen from
as seen from drawing side     completed fabric side

## SEWING

1. Measure the size of square #1 and add at least 3/4" to each dimension for seam allowances. The square in the example below measures 3/4" x 3/4". Cut fabric squares a minimum of 3/4" plus 3/4", or a total of 1 1/2" x 1 1/2". I say "minimum" because you can cut the pieces even larger. Simply trim the seam allowances to 1/4" after sewing each successive seam. For angled pieces (triangles and unusual shapes), add a total of 3/4" to 1" for seam allowances. This ensures the piece will cover the area after it is sewn and opened up.

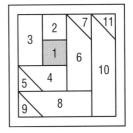

2. Always cut the fabric pieces with the wrong side of the fabric facing up since you will be sewing them right side up to the blank side of the foundation. If you don't do this, you will end up with pieces that are mirror images of the shapes you need. I realize that this makes no difference for symmetrically shaped pieces such as squares and rectangles, but it is a good routine to get into so that when you do cut asymmetrical pieces, they will come out right.

3. Place the fabric for piece #1 right side up on the blank side of the paper so that it covers the area marked "1" and extends at least ¼" beyond the pattern lines on all sides. The numbers will appear reversed. If copy paper is used, hold the piece up to a light source to make placement easier.

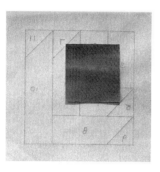

4. Place piece #2 on top of piece #1, right sides together; make sure both fabrics extend at least ¼" beyond the lines. Pin in place.

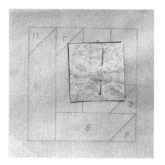

## TIP

To make sure the piece is placed correctly and is large enough, grasp both fabrics along the seam allowance and open up piece #2. It should cover the area marked "2" plus ¼" for seam allowances.

5. Holding the fabrics in place, lay the paper, marked side up, under the presser foot and sew along the seam line between pieces #1 and #2. Extend the stitching a few stitches beyond the beginning and the end of the line.

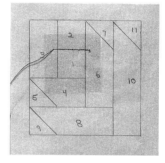

6. Trim the seam allowances to ¼" from the sewn seam. Open up piece #2 and finger-press in place by running your fingers across the seam. (You can also glide the side of the Hera Fabric Marker across the seam.) Press with a dry iron on a cotton setting.

To cut two oversize half-square triangles (the straight grain will be on the short side of the triangle), cut a square 1¼" larger than the short side measurement and cut the square once diagonally. For example, in this block, triangles #5, #7, #9, and #11 measure ¾" along the short side. A 2" square cut once diagonally will provide two oversize triangles of more than adequate size.

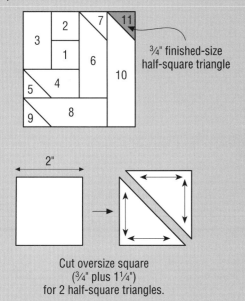

¾" finished-size half-square triangle

2"

Cut oversize square
(¾" plus 1¼")
for 2 half-square triangles.

To cut four oversize quarter-square triangles (with the straight grain on the long side of the triangle), cut a square 1½" larger than the long side of the triangle and cut the square twice diagonally.

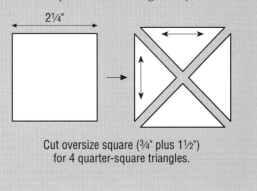

2¼"

Cut oversize square (¾" plus 1½")
for 4 quarter-square triangles.

7. Lay piece #3 across the first two pieces, right sides together. Sew the seam line between pieces #1/#2 and #3. Trim seam allowances to ¼"; open up and finger-press.

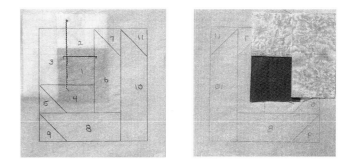

8. Cut a rectangle for piece #4 and add it. There is no need to cut the angled point as it will be created automatically when you add the triangle in the #5 position.

9. Continue to add pieces in sequence until the block is complete. Using the rotary cutter and Bias Square, trim the excess fabric and paper ¼" from the outside pattern lines.

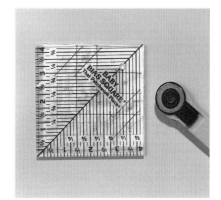

10. Keep the paper intact until you have sewn the paper-pieced block to the surrounding fabric pieces. The sewing line on the pattern provides accuracy and the paper provides stability. After the block is surrounded by other pieces, remove the paper by gently tugging on the seams and tearing it away.

I have included some new two-section block designs that I really like using in my vests. The two-section block designs are made from two paper-pieced triangle sections that are joined diagonally through the middle to form the block.

Machine baste the center seam and check for a good match before you sew the halves together permanently. Press the center seam open to reduce bulk.

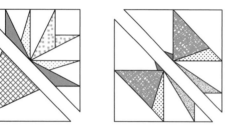

Piece two triangular sections
as separate units and join to form block.

---

# TIP

When sewing paper-pieced patchwork to fabric strips or squares, adjust the stitch length on the sewing machine to 18 to 20 stitches per inch as you sew across the paper, then switch back to the normal stitch length of 12 stitches per inch as you sew fabric to fabric.

---

For many more tips about machine paper piecing and sixty-five designs to paper piece, refer to my book *Easy Machine Paper Piecing*.

## Placing the Squares

Just as there were several options for placing strips on a foundation, there are many options for combining fabric squares and machine paper-pieced patchwork blocks to create a new fabric. Fabric squares can be placed diagonally with paper-pieced blocks running down the center. Squares can be placed in a straight set with a row of paper-pieced blocks or alternating paper-pieced blocks. Of course, fabric squares alone, either straight set or on the diagonal, are also an option. The following examples are some of the placement possibilities. The vest outline in the illustrations shows how a size small might be cut from the sewn squares. Of course, the same concept can be used on both the right and left fronts. For medium and large vest patterns, simply add extra rows or squares as needed.

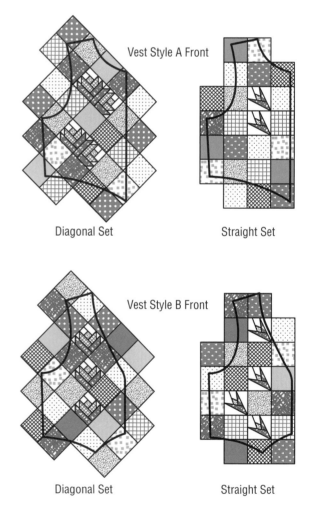

Four Placement Options for Paper-Pieced Blocks and Squares

## Sewing the Squares

*To join squares into a new fabric:*

1. If you have been using a pattern piece that is not transparent up to this point, make a tracing paper or tissue pattern that you can see through.

2. Place the pattern piece right side up on the table. Place your paper-pieced blocks (if any) in the desired location right side up on top of the pattern.

3. Fill in with same-size fabric squares, overlapping them slightly to account for the 1/4"-wide seam allowances until the entire pattern is covered.

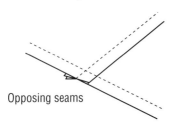

Place squares on right side of pattern piece to determine approximate placement and number of rows needed.

4. Sew the squares into rows, beginning with the longest row. Check the length of each row you sew against the pattern piece and add additional squares if necessary.

5. Press the seam allowances in opposite directions from row to row so they will "lock" when the rows are joined.

Opposing seams

6. Join rows until the sewn unit is large enough to accommodate the pattern piece. If, after sewing 2 rows together, you find you need to add another square to the end of one, just undo the last few stitches, add the square, and restitch.

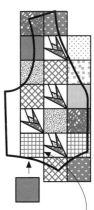

Undo these stitches to join one more square.

7. Place the transparent pattern, right side up, on the right side of the patchwork. Pin in place, aligning the patchwork as you would like. Cut out the pattern piece.

---

## TIP

If you are piecing squares on the diagonal for two vest fronts and you want the squares on both fronts to be at the same angle, draw a pencil line on the transparent pattern front that coincides with one of the diagonal seam lines in the completed patchwork. When you are ready to cut out the other vest front, position the pencil line along a diagonal seam line.

---

Note: When choosing techniques for a reversible vest, avoid lining a diagonally pieced vest section with another diagonally pieced section (for instance, the right front of one vest and the left front of the other vest). This would leave two unsupported bias edges along the front seam.

# Technique 3— Combining Strips, Squares, and Blocks on a Foundation

You can sew strips, squares, and paper-pieced blocks together on a foundation to create still more design options.

## Framing Paper-Pieced Blocks

It is easiest to remove the paper from paper-pieced blocks before attaching them to the foundation, but the block has to be joined to other pieces of fabric on all four sides first. One way to secure the edges of a paper-pieced block is to add fabric strips or triangles around the perimeter.

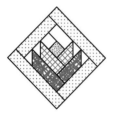  

Paper-Pieced Block
with Fabric Strips

Paper-Pieced Block
with Fabric Triangles

## TIP

To cut the correct-size framing triangles including ¼"-wide seam allowances, divide the finished size of the pieced block by 1.4142 and add ⅞". Cut a square that size and cut once diagonally to make two triangles. For example, a 3" finished paper-pieced block divided by 1.4142 equals 2⅛". Add ⅞" for a total of 3". Cut 2 squares, each 3" x 3", and cut each once diagonally to yield 4 corner triangles. For a 6" finished paper-pieced block, cut the squares 5⅛" x 5⅛"; cut once diagonally for corner triangles.

3"

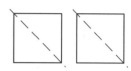

3" square ÷ 1.4142 = 2.12 or 2⅛"

2⅛" + ⅞" (for seam allowances) = 3"

  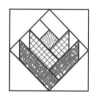

Sew triangles to sides
of center square.

Another way to secure the edges of a paper-pieced block is to incorporate it into the first pieced strip before you attach it to the foundation.

1. Place one or more joined paper-pieced blocks on the foundation in the desired location and angle.

2. Generously estimate the length of fabric needed on each side to cover the foundation. Be especially generous with diagonal patchwork because the angles can be deceiving.

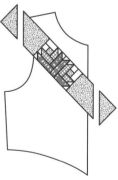

Trim strip generously to coincide
with 2 diagonal edges.

3. Sew the pieces of fabric to each side.
4. Lay the pieced strip back on the foundation and estimate the length of the fabric strips to be added above and below.
5. Add these strips to the pieced strip.

Add a fabric strip on
each side of pieced unit.

6. You can now safely remove the paper from the paper-pieced block.

Note: This method also works for two adjacent strips with paper-pieced blocks. To join two strips, make the top strip first and position it on the foundation to estimate the length of the second strip. Make the second strip, join it to the first, and add plain strips above and below.

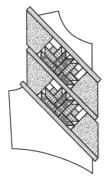

Alternate two rows of
paper-pieced blocks
with plain strips.

7. After you remove the paper, position the pieced unit on the foundation and foundation-piece additional strips above and below until the foundation is covered.

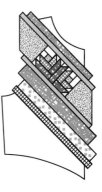

Sometimes you might want to piece your vest in a way that is not conducive to framing. It is possible to add a paper-pieced block directly to the foundation without framing it first. Leave the paper on the block. As you foundation-piece around the block, remove the paper from the seam allowance as soon as you sew each seam. Only the paper in the center of the block will remain. Once foundation piecing is complete, carefully slit the foundation behind the paper-pieced block and remove the paper.

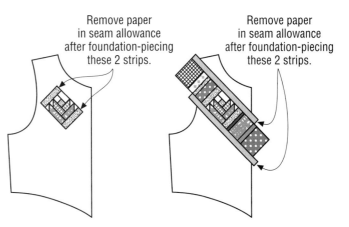

Remove paper in seam allowance after foundation-piecing these 2 strips.

Remove paper in seam allowance after foundation-piecing these 2 strips.

Foundation-piece strips diagonally to left and right of paper-pieced blocks and then above and below.

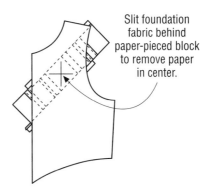

Slit foundation fabric behind paper-pieced block to remove paper in center.

## Placing Strips, Squares, and Paper-Pieced Blocks

Strips of squares, with or without paper-pieced blocks, can be placed vertically or diagonally on the foundation between alternating solid fabric strips. The following are some of the options you have for placing seams and squares in alternating rows. (For more, refer to "Adding Pieced Strips" on page 14.)

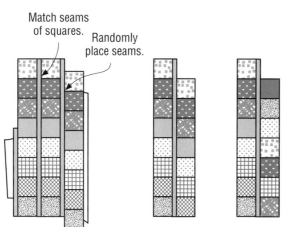

Match seams of squares.

Randomly place seams.

Squares can be joined in same fabric sequence or in random fabric sequence.

You can incorporate paper-pieced patchwork blocks into the pieced strip of squares if the block is the same size as the squares. Prior to foundation piecing, attach solid fabric strips to the long sides of the pieced strip containing the paper-pieced block so you can remove the paper. (See "Framing Paper-Pieced Blocks," beginning on page 26.)

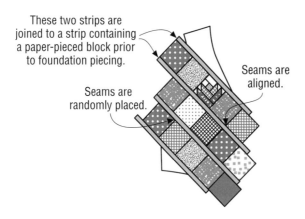

These two strips are joined to a strip containing a paper-pieced block prior to foundation piecing.

Seams are randomly placed.

Seams are aligned.

Solid fabric strips can be foundation-pieced around, above, or below a piece of fabric or a pieced unit. In the illustration below, strips have been foundation-pieced around a diagonally placed block, Log Cabin style.

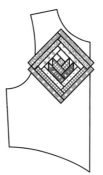

First, attach strips of fabric around paper-pieced block and remove paper. Then position framed block on foundation and foundation-piece subsequent strips in Log Cabin fashion.

Strips can be all the same width or of various widths, as long as the strips in each row are the same width. The size of the strips can play an important part in the design as well.

Draw parallel stop-sewing lines even with the point of the block and foundation-piece strips above and below the block. Remember to remove the paper in the seam allowances of the first round of strips. Slit the back of the foundation to remove the paper behind the block. (See page 27.)

Stop-sewing lines

Foundation-piece vertical strips to the left and right of the block to cover the foundation.

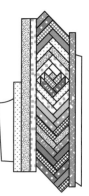

Just as with the other techniques, there are many design options available when you combine strips, paper-pieced blocks, and squares on a foundation. The following are two more examples of designs combining paper-pieced blocks and strips on a foundation.

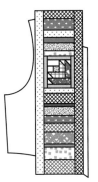

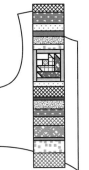

Draw stop-sewing lines on foundation parallel with outside edge of framed paper-pieced block.

Foundation-piece horizontal strips.

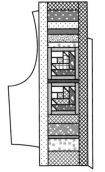

Foundation-piece vertical strips.

Foundation-piece 2 joined paper-pieced blocks in the same manner.

Though all the examples thus far have used the vest front pattern pieces, you can use any of the techniques on the back of the vest as well. Since the back is a larger area, a single 6" paper-pieced block or four 3" paper-pieced blocks joined to make a 6" square work well. One idea is to center a square on the vest back foundation and frame it with diagonal, vertical, and/or horizontal strips.

The first example shows a pieced block set on point. The four corner triangles create a straight-set square so that strips can be added to the sides, top, and bottom.

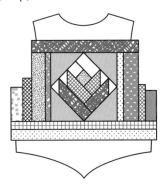

Frame paper-pieced block with triangles before placing on foundation.

The second example shows four 3" Butterfly blocks joined to make a 6" square. The four-block unit was then framed by strips and the paper removed. Strips were foundation-pieced above and below the block and then to the right and left to cover the foundation.

If you forget to remove the paper or prefer to leave it on while you sew the paper-pieced block to the foundation, use the technique described on page 27 to remove the paper.

Once the foundation has been completely covered with blocks, squares, and/or strips, trim the patchwork around the outside edges of the foundation.

# Embellishments

mbellishments add detail and interest. When I wear my vests, people often notice the embellishments first because they provide that little extra touch that make the vest special. The following are just a few ideas to consider.

## Prairie Points

Prairie points are quick and easy to make and they provide delightful detail. Fold squares of fabric into a triangle and insert them into a seam before stitching. The points will face in the opposite direction of the strips being added. Adding strips to the right will give you points that face left. Adding strips in an upward direction will give you points that face down.

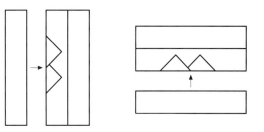

Prairie points added to strips that are being stitched to the foundation from the top down will point up and may droop. Secure the tips by tacking them with a stitch. You can also add a small bead as an embellishment when you tack the points. Do this before joining two sides of the vest if you are making a reversible vest.

*To make prairie points, cut a 2" square of fabric and fold it in one of the following ways:*

• Fold the square in half diagonally, wrong sides together, and press. Fold in half again, matching the points along the long side, and press. This method allows you to overlap points by slipping one point slightly inside the one next to it.

One point slipped
inside the other

• For a center welt, fold the square wrong sides together into a rectangle and press. Bring the corners of the long folded edge down until they meet in the center of the long cut edge. Press. Position with the center welt either showing or facing down.

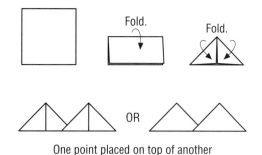
One point placed on top of another

*To add a prairie point to strips being sewn to a foundation:*

1. Position the raw edge of the point along the raw edge of the last strip you added. Baste in place 1/8" from the edge. A prairie point can be made smaller by adjusting it within the seam allowance of the strip and cutting away the excess on the long side.
2. Sew the next strip to secure the point.

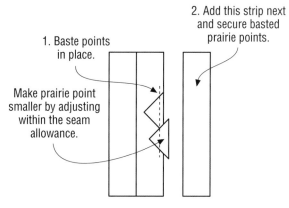

Prairie points can also be added between seamed squares or rows of squares. Machine baste the folded prairie point right side up on the right side of the square edge and stitch in place when the next square or row is joined.

# Decorative Topstitching

The wonderful decorative stitches now available on many sewing machines are another great way to embellish your vest. Decorative stitching can be added along the seam lines between fabric strips or through the middle of fabric strips that have been sewn to the foundation before the two vest sides are joined. The foundation supports the fabric and keeps it smooth as you embroider. Use a commercial tear-away or piece of paper to support the fabric when you machine embroider a single layer of fabric. The Fancy Turquoise Vest on page 37 has topstitching along the seams and in the middle of some of the strips.

Many decorative threads that can enhance machine embroidery are now available. Machine-embroidery thread is available in a wide variety of colors. Metallic threads are wonderful for a glittery or a dressy look; be sure to use special topstitch sewing-machine needles. The Hearts and Flowers vest on page 38 has metallic gold topstitching.

Test decorative stitches with the intended threads on scraps of similar fabrics first to confirm your choices. When you complete the embroidery, pull the top threads to the back by tugging on the bobbin thread at the beginning and end of the line of stitching. Tie the ends together, then thread a needle with the tails and weave them back into the fabric.

# Fabric Manipulations

Fabric manipulations, such as pintucking or pleating, can also enhance portions of your vest. Make a piece of fabric using the desired manipulation, then cut it to size and add it to the vest.

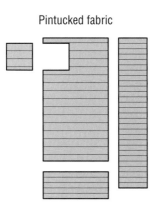

Pintucked fabric

Strips, both vertical and horizontal, and squares can be used in your vest.

# Ribbons and Lace

Embroidered ribbons, shiny ribbons, and decorative laces can add a special touch to your vest. If you sew strips to a foundation, you can use ribbon strips instead of fabric strips. When selecting ribbons for this purpose, keep in mind that the seam allowances will take up ¼" on each long side of the ribbon.

Another option is to topstitch the ribbon on one or both sides rather than sewing it into a seam. Lay the ribbon edge right side up on top of the edge of the strip before it and topstitch. Join to the next strip the same way. This technique is helpful when you don't want to lose a decorative ribbon edge, or when the ribbon is heavy and would create excess bulk in a seam allowance. The ribbon may also be topstitched across foundation-pieced fabrics as a decoration.

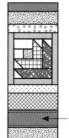

— Ribbon

Strips of lace can be added in a number of ways. Insert the lace between two strips of fabric before sewing them together. This is similar to the way in which prairie points are added; the lace will be free along one edge. Another option is to machine baste a strip of lace on top of a fabric strip of the same width and treat it as one unit. Sew lace strips and motifs onto your vest before you join the two sides of a reversible vest.

# Trinkets, Baubles, and Beads

Embellishments such as small charms, bits of costume jewelry, beads, and specialty buttons can give your vest a wonderful personality or "look." Use beads as an accent or to tack down another embellishment. For instance, the pointed edges of a decorative piece of lace can be secured with beads after it has been stitched between two fabric strips. Be sure to add these embellishments to your vest before joining the sides.

# Shoulder Accents

Ruffled or pleated shoulder accents add width to the shoulder area and are very flattering on some figures. Insert shoulder accents when you sew the two sides of the reversible vest together.

To make ruffles and pleats, select a fabric that goes well with both sides of the reversible vest. Width and length are flexible.

1. Cut 2 fabric strips, each 3 times the length of the area you want to cover plus $\frac{1}{2}$", and twice the width plus $\frac{3}{4}$". For example, cut $15\frac{1}{2}$" long to cover a 5" length (3" x 5" + $\frac{1}{2}$"), and $3\frac{1}{4}$" wide for a $1\frac{1}{4}$" finished width ($1\frac{1}{4}$" x 2 + $\frac{3}{4}$").
2. Fold each strip in half lengthwise, right sides together, and sew a $\frac{1}{4}$"-wide seam on each short end.
3. Clip the corners, turn the strips right side out, and press, aligning the long cut sides.

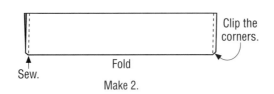

Make 2.

You can also sew two different fabrics together. This allows the shoulder accent fabric to be different on the reverse side. Since bits of the other side may be visible, only use this option when the fabrics on the two sides of the shoulder accent are of similar values and/or compatible colors.

1. Cut 2 strips of each fabric. Strips should measure 3 times the length plus $\frac{1}{2}$" by the finished width plus $\frac{5}{8}$". Strips for the ruffles on the Hearts and Flowers vest on page 38 were each cut $2\frac{1}{2}$" x $15\frac{1}{2}$".
2. Layer 2 strips, 1 of each different fabric, right sides together. Sew around 3 sides as shown, using a $\frac{1}{4}$" -wide seam allowance.
3. Clip the corners, turn right side out, and press. Repeat for the other shoulder accent.

Join 2 different fabrics to make shoulder accent different on each vest side.

Optional: Topstitch around the edges to add definition.

To make ruffles, sew a long running stitch with the machine or by hand $\frac{1}{8}$" from the long cut edges (or the unsewn edges of a two-fabric ruffle). Pull the thread to gather the fabric to the desired length. Position the gathered strip at the shoulder and baste in place as described below.

To make pleats, fold the strip into pleats, pin, and steam press into place. Machine baste $\frac{1}{8}$" from the unsewn edges. Position the pleated strip at the shoulder and baste in place as described below.

*To attach the ruffle or pleated strip:*
1. Fold the ruffle or pleated strip in half crosswise to locate the midpoint. Match the midpoint to the vest shoulder seam.
2. Pin the raw edges of the ruffle or pleated strip flush with the raw edge of the vest shoulder and machine baste in place $\frac{1}{8}$" from the edge.

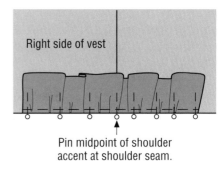

Pin midpoint of shoulder accent at shoulder seam.

The strip will be sewn in place when you sew the two sides of the reversible vest together.

# Two Vests for the Price of One

You now know everything you need to know to make a unique and attractive patchwork vest. All you have to decide is which colors, fabrics, and techniques you would like to use on your own vest!

When I made my first patchwork vests using conventional methods, I felt bound to use the same patchwork technique for both the right front, left front, and back. I now consider each vest section as an opportunity to combine patchwork techniques and fabrics for an interesting coordinated look. The reverse vest can have a whole new look when you keep in mind the following two considerations.

1. The issue of color discussed on pages 6–9.
2. If I plan on foundation-piecing one of the fronts on each vest, I make sure that the two foundations don't end up on the same side once the vests are joined. If I am going to foundation-piece the right front of one vest, I foundation-piece the right front of the reverse vest as well. This way each foundation is lined with a single layer and both front sections have the same weight.

The Gallery of Vests contains color photos of the vests with instructions in this book. Browse among them and choose two for your vest. If you want to save time and prefer not to make two full-fledged patchwork vest sides, here are some ideas for making the second side out of whole pieces of fabric:

- Use a pretty floral chintz, exciting paisley, or any other fabric that appeals to you.
- Use a small-scale fabric for the back and a larger-scale coordinating fabric for the fronts.
- Use a large-scale fabric for the back and a smaller-scale fabric for the fronts.
- Use a small stripe for the back, a larger-scale, blending-type fabric for one front, and a matching small-scale print for the other front.

# Reversible Vests

# Gallery of Vests

## Blue, Blue Waves

*By Carol Doak, 1994, Windham, New Hampshire. Decorative machine stitching along several seam lines and dressy buttons add extra detail and interest to this two-way strip-pieced vest. The medium values placed at the shoulders and the darker values placed in the lower portion provide a figure-flattering design. Directions on page 51.*

## Something Blue ➣

*By Carol Doak, 1994, Windham, New Hampshire. The reversible side of the Something Old wedding vest on page 38 makes a great "going-away" vest. Silver and blue fabrics are strip-pieced in Log Cabin fashion around the Heart and Flower paper-pieced block. The other vest front is strip pieced vertically and includes prairie-point accents and a silver embossed ribbon. Directions on page 65.*

## ➣ Emeralds and Sapphires

*By Carol Doak, 1994, Windham, New Hampshire. The clear blues and greens grouped together for this vest are reminiscent of gemstones. The rotated paper-pieced geometric blocks placed in the diagonal strip are quite subtle except for the dramatic metallic gold rays. Directions on page 55.*

## ⤝ Blue Birds of Paradise

*By Carol Doak, 1994, Windham, New Hampshire. The subtle Yukata fabric with flying birds and thin, brush stroke–type grass sets the theme for this vest. The strip-pieced patchwork side features an undercurrent of blue fabrics, alternating with navy blue polished-cotton strips. Directions on page 56.*

## Blue and Purple Passions ➤

*By Carol Doak, 1993, Windham, New Hampshire. The Yukata Japanese floral creates a striking image by combining colors that you might not ordinarily put together. The remainder of the fabrics for this vest are grouped around the blues, purples, and coral accent. The paper-pieced Flower block creates a subtle detail on the strip-pieced front. Directions on page 66.*

## ⤝ Oriental Tea Garden

*By Carol Doak, 1994, Windham, New Hampshire. Fabrics in this vest were chosen to coordinate with the large-scale Oriental-style print. The gray patchwork squares and the variety of colors in the paper-pieced blocks allow this vest to go with several different pieces of clothing. Directions on page 52.*

## Madam Butterfly

*By Carol Doak, 1994, Windham, New Hampshire. The medium-scale print used in the strips on the front was the inspiration for choosing a variety of black, gray, and metallic gold fabrics for the diagonally cut alternate strips. On the back, four Butterfly blocks are rotated to create a dramatic star design. Made of lamé and black polished cotton, the design is framed with black satin. The rest of the back is foundation-pieced using strips of black-and-gold fabrics. A single strip of black ribbon with an embroidered metallic gold pattern is topstitched horizontally above the block. Directions on page 62.*

## Red Hot Strippers

*By Carol Doak, 1994, Windham, New Hampshire. The variety of red fabrics in this vest allows it to coordinate with several different shades of red clothing. The small amounts of black polished cotton provide an accent. Directions on page 50.*

## Fancy Turquoise

*By Carol Doak, 1994, Windham, New Hampshire. This vest was made to go with clothing in a hard-to-match olive green. The subtle and flowing turquoise print, containing several different olive greens, was the answer. Decorative stitching along the diagonal seam lines adds detail. Directions on page 58.*

## Morning Glory

*By Carol Doak, 1994, Windham, New Hampshire. The striking Yukata floral sets the color and theme for this vest. The medium blue fabric strips are concentrated in the upper portion, and the darker blue strips in the lower portion. The two paper-pieced flower blocks worked in lighter blues and pink add interest and continue the theme. Directions on page 67.*

## Hearts and Flowers

*By Carol Doak, 1994, Windham, New Hampshire. The green floral chintz sets a romantic theme for this vest. The Heart and Flower paper-pieced block and the lace appliqués carry the theme through on the other front and on the vest back. Tiny pink beads decorate each lace heart appliqué. Decorative stitching along some of the seam lines adds just a touch of "glitz." The shoulder ruffles complete the picture for a soft and feminine vest. Directions on page 68.*

## Something Old

*By Carol Doak, 1994, Windham, New Hampshire. Several white and ecru fabrics were used for this stunning wedding vest. Stitched pintucking on three of these fabrics adds detail. The paper-pieced Nosegay block along with lace, satin, metallic ribbons, appliqués, and tiny pearls provide just the right touches for the wedding theme. Directions on page 60.*

# Sunny Spring

*By Carol Doak, 1994, Windham, New Hampshire. The large-scale floral was the inspiration for grouping soft yellows and greens for the patchwork side of this vest. The paper-pieced Nosegay blocks, set against a white background, continue the pink and green color scheme. Directions on page 53.*

# Springtime Tulips

*By Carol Doak, 1993, Windham, New Hampshire. This vest was made to go with a variety of white and off-white summer clothing. The pink and green scraps used in the paper-pieced blocks also coordinate with a variety of clothing pieces in those two colors. The small-scale rosebud print used for the background in the paper-pieced blocks also appears on the back of the vest. Directions on page 54.*

# Vests for Inspiration

 he vests on the next several pages do not have specific instructions; they are shown here for inspiration only. As you can see from the wide range of fabrics chosen and techniques used, the creative possibilities are endless. And if you're like me, once you get started, you won't be able to stop yourself.

Note: Some of the vests pictured in this section were made using a commercial pattern.

## Vest 1
*By Carol Doak, 1994, Windham, New Hampshire.*

## Vest 2
*By Carol Doak, 1994, Windham, New Hampshire.*

## Vest 3
*By Carol Doak, 1994, Windham, New Hampshire.*

## Vest 4

*By Ginny Guaraldi, 1994,*
*Londonderry, New Hampshire.*

## Vest 5

*By Carol Doak, 1994,*
*Windham, New Hampshire.*

## Vest 6

*By Carol Boer, 1994,*
*Woodinville, Washington.*

## Vest 7
*By Pam Ludwig, 1994,*
*Windham, New Hampshire.*

## Vest 8
*By Ginny Guaraldi, 1994,*
*Londonderry, New Hampshire.*

## Vest 9
*By Carol Doak, 1993,*
*Windham, New Hampshire.*

## Vest 10
*By Carol Doak, 1994,*
*Windham, New Hampshire.*

## Vest 11
*By Carol Doak, 1994,*
*Windham, New Hampshire.*

## Vest 12
*By Moira Clegg, 1994,*
*Windham, New Hampshire.*

## Vest 13
*By Carol Doak, 1994,*
*Windham, New Hampshire.*

## Vest 14
*By Carol Doak, 1994,*
*Windham, New Hampshire.*

## Vest 15
*By Carol Doak, 1994,*
*Windham, New Hampshire.*

## Vest 16

*By Carol Doak, 1994,*
*Windham, New Hampshire.*

## Vest 17

*By Carol Doak, 1994,*
*Windham, New Hampshire.*

## Vest 18

*By Terry Maddox, 1994,*
*Pelham, New Hampshire.*

**Vest 19**
*By Roxanne Carter, 1994,*
*Mukilteo, Washington.*

**Vest 20**
*By Roxanne Carter, 1994,*
*Mukilteo, Washington.*

**Vest 21**
*By Carol Doak, 1994,*
*Windham, New Hampshire.*

## Vest 22

*By Carol Doak, 1994,*
*Windham, New Hampshire.*

## Vest 23

*By Carol Doak, 1994,*
*Windham, New Hampshire.*

## Vest 24

*By Beckie Hansen, 1994,*
*Mukilteo, Washington.*

## Vest 25
*By Carol Doak, 1994,*
*Windham, New Hampshire.*

## Vest 26
*By Carol Doak, 1994,*
*Windham, New Hampshire.*

## Vest 27
*By Carol Doak, 1994,*
*Windham, New Hampshire.*

he vest sides presented in this section are offered as suggestions for grouping fabrics and choosing from the techniques described earlier. It is important to read all of the instructional sections before making these vests. Any technique can be used in conjunction with any vest pattern. Use these vest suggestions as presented or as the basis or inspiration for your own design.

Directions for each vest side include the vest pattern style pictured; the color, type, and amount of fabric used; and cutting and piecing information. The number of strips or squares indicated will be enough for a size small of that vest style. If you are making a larger size or a different style, cut additional strips or squares from the yardage as needed.

Note: Yardage requirements for the fabrics used in the following vest patterns are based on 44"-wide fabric, except for the requirements for Yukata fabrics, which are based on 15"-wide fabric.

When a vest design features a large-scale print or Japanese Yukata fabric, move the transparent pattern piece around on the fabric to determine the best use of the print before cutting out the pattern.

Feel free to combine any of the vest sides in your reversible vest. The originals don't even have to be from the same pattern (Vest Style A), as the techniques are easy to convert from one vest style to the other by arranging the patchwork elements a little differently or cutting and sewing more or fewer fabric strips or squares. You do, of course, need to use the same vest pattern for both sides of your reversible vest.

For more specific instructions on the various techniques you want to use, refer to the appropriate section in "Piecing Techniques," beginning on page 10. Once you have pieced your vest sides, see "Assembly and Finishing" on page 70 to complete your vest.

Yardage requirements for pieced sections are not hard and fast. They only provide a concept of the number of fabrics needed and their relative amounts. I call for 1/8 yard of many fabrics because that is the minimum cut most stores will make. If you already have some fabric on hand, you can probably get by with less in the smaller vest sizes. I do call for scraps when just a tiny amount of fabric is needed, as for paper-pieced blocks. Use more or fewer fabrics than indicated, according to your preference and the yardage available to you.

Yardage requirements for one-piece sections are less flexible. They depend on the size and style of your vest. I cut one-piece sections on the lengthwise grain of the fabric so that the slight stretch in the crosswise grain falls on the width of the garment. The chart on page 10 gives the amount you need for any one-piece section in the three vest styles in this book. To calculate the amount you need for a purchased vest pattern, measure the pattern from shoulder to hem, including seam allowances, and buy enough fabric to accommodate the pattern piece lengthwise.

If you really want to use a certain piece of fabric, and it's not large enough for the pattern piece, feel free to join additional fabrics to it—these are patchwork vests, after all!

Note: Many of the vests call for strips cut from the fabrics that remain after one-piece sections are cut. If you are making a large-size vest, you may need to cut more short strips and piece them.

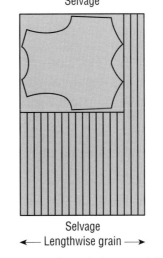

Selvage

Selvage

◄— Lengthwise grain —►

Cut strips on crosswise grain from remaining fabric.
Piece if necessary for desired length.

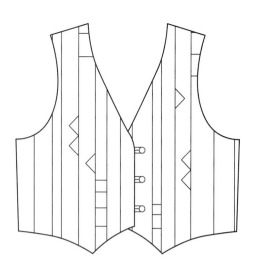

# VEST FACTS

**Technique 1
Page 11**

**Color photo: page 36
Vest Style B Option**

**Fabrics:** Eight prints in reds and red and black with a slight change in value are used for the fronts. Use a solid black polished cotton as an accent. The main-player fabric (also used on the back) is a large-scale red-and-black print.

## Materials: 44"-wide fabrics

**Back:** ¾ yd.* large-scale red-and-black print
**Foundation:** ¾ yd.* dark cotton (2 fronts)
**Fronts:** ⅛ yd. each of 8 red and red-and-black prints and ⅛ yd. black polished cotton

*Vest Style B Option, size small. Refer to the chart on page 10 for other styles and sizes.

## Cutting and Piecing

*Cut additional strips as needed if you are making a larger size or a different style.*
1. Cut out the back.
2. Cut out a left and a right front foundation.
3. Cut 1 strip, 1¼" wide, from the black polished cotton.

4. From the 8 red and black fabrics and the remaining back fabric, cut the following for a total of 9 strips:
   - 3 strips, each 1½" wide
   - 3 strips, each 1¾" wide
   - 3 strips, each 2" wide
5. Cut a 9" segment from each of the following strips for a total of 4 segments of 4 different fabrics:
   - 2 of the 1½" strips
   - 1 of the 1¾" strips
   - 1 of the 2" strips
6. Sew these 9" strips together as shown and cut 5 segments as indicated.
   - 3 segments, each 1½" wide
   - 1 segment, 1¾" wide
   - 1 segment, 2" wide

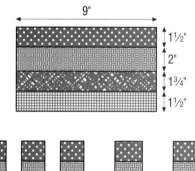

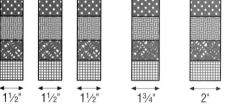

7. Make 6 black polished-cotton prairie points from 2" squares. (See page 30.)
8. Begin with either the right or left front foundation and position the single-fabric strips vertically. Insert the 5 pieced segments, sewing them at random in the middle of a strip of the same width (or at either end). Foundation-piece the strips, adding the prairie points randomly. Include one strip of the black polished-cotton accent fabric. Complete the other vest front in the same manner.
9. For "Assembly and Finishing," see pages 70–74.

## Vest Facts

**Technique 1
Page 11**

**Color photo: page 34
Vest Style B Option**

**Fabrics:** Eight different blue prints, ranging from medium blue to very dark blue, are used for the fronts. A solid blue polished cotton acts as an accent. Select a medium-scale dark blue print for the back.

## Materials: 44"-wide fabrics

**Back:** ¾ yd.* medium-scale dark blue print
**Foundation:** ¾ yd.* dark cotton (2 fronts)
**Fronts:** ⅛ yd. each of 8 different blue prints in a range of medium to dark values and ⅛ yd. medium blue polished cotton

*Vest Style B Option, size small. Refer to the chart on page 10 for other styles and sizes.

## Cutting and Piecing

*Cut additional strips as needed if you are making a larger size or a different style.*

1. Cut out the back.
2. Cut out a left front and right front foundation. Mark them "right" and "left." Lay one foundation on top of the other, right sides together. Use a Hera fabric marker to make a diagonal crease across both foundations from the armhole down to the center front. This will be the stop-sewing line for the first set of pieced strips. (See the illustration on page 19.)
3. From the blue polished cotton, cut 2 strips, each 1¼" wide.
4. From each of the 4 lightest blues, cut 1 strip, ranging from 1¼" to 2" wide. From the 4 remaining blues and the remaining back fabric, cut a total of 6 strips, ranging from 1¼" to 2" wide. (Cut 2 strips from one of the fabrics.)
5. Begin foundation piecing with the lighter blue strips in the upper section of each front. Stop sewing at the line. (See page 19.) Piece both upper fronts at the same time.
6. Continue with the darker blue strips, placing the first one diagonally across the bottom edge of the upper pieced section. Include the darkest of the fabrics from the light group. Complete the other front in a similar manner.

   Optional: To add detail, sew a variety of decorative machine stitches in light blue thread along several of the seam lines.

7. For "Assembly and Finishing," see pages 70–74.

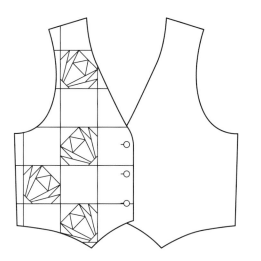

## VEST FACTS

| Technique 2 Page 20 | **Color photo: page 35**<br>**Vest Style B Option** |

**Fabrics:** The large-scale floral print is the main-player fabric. Five gray fabrics with similar values are used for the patchwork squares. A small-scale black print forms the background of the paper-pieced blocks, and a variety of scraps in blue, green, pink, and silver are used for the rays. The vest back is a subtle black-and-gray print.

## Materials: 44"-wide fabrics

**Back:** ³⁄₄ yd.* subtle black-and-gray print
**Left Front:** ³⁄₄ yd.* large-scale floral print
**Right Front:** Scraps (at least 3½" x 3½") of 5 different gray prints (approximately ½ yd. total)
**Paper-Pieced Blocks:** ⅛ yd. small-scale black print and a variety of scraps in blue, green, pink, and silver (⅛ yd. total)

*Vest Style B Option, size small. Refer to the chart on page 10 for other styles and sizes.

## Cutting and Piecing

*Cut additional squares as needed if you are making a larger size or a different style.*

1. Cut out the back.
2. Cut out the left front.
3. From the 5 gray prints, cut a total of 21 squares, each 3½" x 3½".
4. Paper-piece 4 Geometric Block #19. Use the black print for the backgrounds, but make each block different by using a variety of scraps for the other sections.

G19

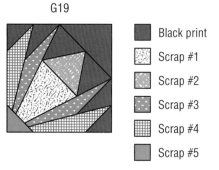

| | Black print |
| --- | --- |
| | Scrap #1 |
| | Scrap #2 |
| | Scrap #3 |
| | Scrap #4 |
| | Scrap #5 |

5. Position the paper-pieced blocks and the gray squares on top of the right front pattern piece in a straight set as shown in the vest plan. Begin piecing the squares together in vertical rows, starting with the longest row. Add rows until the pattern piece is completely covered. Join the rows.
6. Cut out the right front. (See page 25.) Remove the paper from the back of the paper-pieced blocks.
7. For "Assembly and Finishing," see pages 70–74.

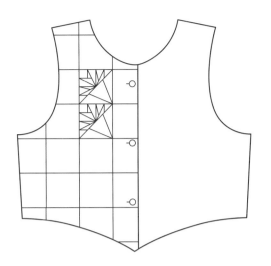

## Cutting and Piecing

*Cut additional squares as needed if you are making a larger size or a different style.*

1. Cut out the back.
2. Cut out the left front.
3. Paper-piece 2 Nosegay blocks (F24). This block is one of the two-section paper-pieced block designs. (See page 24.) Machine baste the center seam and check for a good match before you sew the halves together permanently. Press the center seam open.

F24

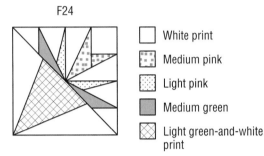

☐ White print

▨ Medium pink

▨ Light pink

▨ Medium green

▨ Light green-and-white print

# Vest Facts

| Technique 2 Page 20 | Color photo: page 39 Vest Style A |

**Fabrics:** The soft yellow floral is both the main-player fabric and the inspiration for this vest. Squares of four other yellow prints with similar values create a subtle background for the paper-pieced blocks. A light green moiré is included for a different texture. Since the yellows are so light, a white print is used for the background of the paper-pieced Nosegay blocks. The flowers themselves are made of slightly darker pinks and greens.

## Materials: 44"-wide fabrics

**Back:** ¾ yd.* light green–and-white print
**Left Front:** ¾ yd.* large-scale yellow floral
**Right Front:** ⅛ yd. light green moiré, and ⅛ yd. each of 4 yellow prints
**Paper-Pieced Blocks:** ⅛ yd. white print, scraps of medium pink, light pink, and medium green

*Vest Style A, size small. Refer to the chart on page 10 for other styles and sizes.

4. From the remaining large-scale yellow floral, the 4 yellow prints, and the green moiré, cut a total of 23 squares, each 3½" x 3½".
5. Position the paper-pieced blocks and the squares on top of the right front pattern piece. Piece the squares in the center vertical row containing the paper-pieced blocks. Continue to join squares to form vertical rows. Add rows until the pattern piece is completely covered. Join the rows.
6. Cut out the right front. (See page 25.) Remove the paper from the back of the paper-pieced blocks.
7. For "Assembly and Finishing," see pages 70–74.

# Springtime Tulips

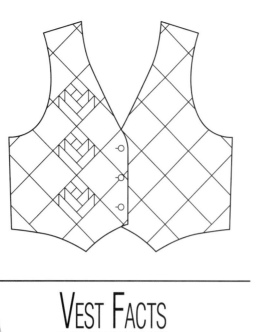

## VEST FACTS

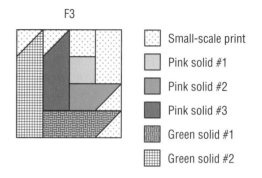

| Technique 2<br>Page 20 | **Color photo: page 39**<br>**Vest Style B** |

**Fabrics:** A variety of white, white-and-green, and white-and-pink prints are grouped for the patchwork squares. A small-scale print of pink flowers on a white background is used for the back. The three paper-pieced Tulip blocks have scraps of solid pinks and solid greens in light to dark values against a background of the print from the back.

## Materials: 44"-wide fabrics

**Back:** ¾ yd.* white print with pink flowers
**Right and Left Fronts:** Scraps (at least 3½" x 3½") of white solid, white-on-white prints, white-and-green prints, and a white-and-pink print (approximately ¾ yd. total for Vests A and B and 1 yd. total for Vest C.)
**Paper-Pieced Blocks:** Small scraps of green and pink solids in light to dark values

*Vest Style B, size small. Refer to the chart on page 10 for other styles and sizes.

## Cutting and Piecing

*Cut additional squares as needed if you are making a larger size or a different style.*
1. Cut out the back.
2. Paper-piece 3 Flower Block #3.

F3

- Small-scale print
- Pink solid #1
- Pink solid #2
- Pink solid #3
- Green solid #1
- Green solid #2

3. From the white solid and the white, green, and pink prints, cut approximately 45 squares, each 3½" x 3½".
4. Position the paper-pieced blocks on top of the right front pattern piece on point in a vertical line as shown in the vest plan and fill in with the cut squares. Sew the squares together in diagonal rows across the longest portion; continue to add rows until the pattern piece is completely covered. Join the rows.
5. Cut out the right front. (See page 25.) Remove the paper from the back of the paper-pieced blocks.
6. For the left front, arrange the remaining print squares on the left front pattern piece diagonally and sew the squares together. Join the rows. Cut out the left front. (See Tip on page 25 for how to keep the diagonal line the same on both fronts.)
7. For "Assembly and Finishing," see pages 70–74.

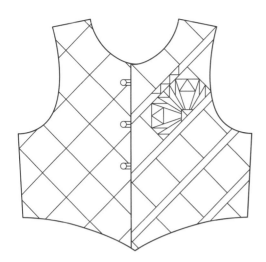

## Cutting and Piecing

1. Cut out the back.
2. Cut out a left front foundation.
3. Paper-piece 2 Geometric Block #19 and join them as shown in the vest plan.

G19

| | |
|---|---|
| ■ | Navy polished cotton |
| ▦ | Blue print #1 |
| ▦ | Blue print #2 |
| ▦ | Metallic gold |
| ▦ | Green print |
| ▦ | Blue print #3 |

4. From each of the blue and green prints and the remaining back fabric (a total of 7 fabrics), cut 1 strip, $3\frac{1}{2}$" x 26". Layer the strips and cut into 7 squares, each $3\frac{1}{2}$" x $3\frac{1}{2}$", for a total of 49 squares. From each of the blue and dark green polished cottons, cut 1 strip, $1\frac{1}{4}$" wide.

5. Position the paper-pieced blocks diagonally on the left front foundation and fill in with the cut squares. Remove the blocks from the foundation and piece squares to the upper right and lower left until the strip covers the foundation. Sew a $1\frac{1}{4}$"-wide green polished cotton strip above and a $1\frac{1}{4}$"-wide blue polished cotton strip below. Watch those angles! Remove the paper.

6. Continue to piece squares together in diagonal rows. Foundation-piece them above and below the paper-pieced strip, alternating with solid polished-cotton strips as shown in the vest plan. Place the seams and fabrics randomly. Insert 3 prairie points in the green strip above the paper-pieced strip. See page 30 for making prairie points.

7. To make the right front, arrange the remaining blue and green squares on top of the right front pattern piece in diagonal rows. Sew the squares together. Continue to add rows until the pattern piece is completely covered. Join the rows. Cut out the right front.

8. For "Assembly and Finishing," see pages 70–74.

## Vest Facts

| Technique 2 Page 20 Technique 3 Page 26 | Color photo: page 34 Vest Style A |
|---|---|

**Fabrics:** For this vest, I grouped three clear blue and three clear green prints in medium to dark values. The back fabric is a subtle dark blue-and-green print. The navy, blue, and dark green polished cottons provide a change in texture. Accents come from the metallic gold stars in one of the blue fabrics and the metallic gold rays in the paper-pieced blocks.

## Materials: 44"-wide fabrics

**Back:** $\frac{3}{4}$ yd.* subtle dark blue–and-green print
**Foundation:** $\frac{3}{4}$ yd.* dark cotton (1 front)
**Right and Left Front:** $\frac{1}{8}$ yd. each of 3 subtle blue and 3 subtle green prints in medium to dark values** and $\frac{1}{8}$ yd. each blue and dark green polished cottons
**Paper-Pieced Blocks:** Small scrap of gold metallic and scrap of navy blue polished cotton

*Vest Style A, size small. Refer to the chart on page 10 for other styles and sizes.

**For Vest C, add one more $\frac{1}{8}$ yard of a subtle blue or green print.

# Blue Birds of Paradise

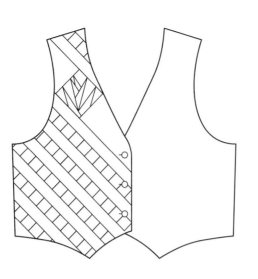

## Vest Facts

Technique 3
Page 26

Color photo: page 35
Vest Style B Option

**Fabrics:** The main-player Yukata fabric is used for the left front of the vest. It features blue birds and black grasses against a slate gray background and sets the theme for this vest. The right side has a floral paper-pieced block set in a diagonal strip. The strip-pieced squares are composed of four blue and black prints in medium dark values and a solid medium blue polished cotton. I usually let the background of the large-scale print dictate color for the patchwork fabrics, but when I tried out slate gray fabrics, this vest seemed dull. I settled on clearer blue fabrics for the patchwork and was pleased with the result. The alternating strip is a navy blue polished cotton, and the Flower block background is a light blue print. I used a small-scale black-and-gray print on the back of the vest.

## Materials: 44"-wide fabrics

**Back:** ³/₄ yd.* small-scale black-and-gray print
**Left Front:** ³/₄ yd.* large-scale Yukata print
**Foundation:** ³/₄ yd.* dark cotton (1 front)
**Right Front:** ¹/₈ yd. each of 4 different blue and black prints, ¹/₈ yd. medium blue polished cotton, and ¹/₄ yd. navy blue polished cotton
**Paper-Pieced Block:** Large scrap of light blue for the background

*Vest Style B Option, size small. Refer to the chart on page 10 for other styles and sizes.

## Cutting and Piecing

*Cut additional strips as needed if you are making a larger size or a different style.*

1. Cut out the back.
2. Cut out the left front.
3. Cut out a right front foundation.
4. Paper-piece 1 Flower Block #10.

F10

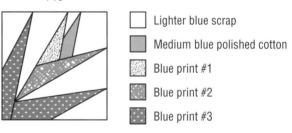

| | Lighter blue scrap |
| | Medium blue polished cotton |
| | Blue print #1 |
| | Blue print #2 |
| | Blue print #3 |

5. Position the paper-pieced block on the right front foundation as shown in the vest plan. Measure the approximate length needed to cover the foundation on either side. See page 26. Remove the block from the foundation. From the remaining back fabric, cut 2 strips, each 3¹/₂" wide and long enough to cover the foundation. Sew strips to the upper left and lower right edges of the block.
6. From the navy blue polished cotton, cut 3 strips, each 1¹/₂" wide.

7. Position the paper-pieced strip on the right front foundation again and measure the length needed for the strips above and below. Remove the paper-pieced strip from the foundation and sew the 1½" navy strips to opposite sides. Remove the paper from the back of the paper-pieced block. Pin the paper-pieced strip in position on the foundation.

8. From each of the 4 different blue and black prints, the medium blue polished cotton, and the remaining back fabric, cut 1 strip, 1½" wide. Sew the strips together along the long edges and press the seam allowances in the same direction. True up one end and cut 12 segments, each 1½" wide. Cut additional segments as needed. See "Making Pieced Strips" on page 14.

9. Join 2 segments (or 3 if necessary) end to end to create a pieced strip long enough to cover the foundation below the paper-pieced strip. Foundation-piece strips of squares, alternating with navy blue polished cotton strips so the seams and fabrics in each pieced strip match the preceding pieced strip. (See page 18 for aligning seams.) Each fabric will appear to run diagonally under the navy blue strips. Continue until the foundation is completely covered both above and below the paper-pieced strip. Watch those angles!

10. For "Assembly and Finishing," see pages 70–74.

---

# TIP

If the piece of Yukata fabric is not long enough to accommodate the pattern piece, you can insert a piece of the excess Yukata fabric or other coordinating fabric in the shoulder area to fill in. To use this trick, place the large print where you want it on the pattern piece and cut out. Join a piece of fabric to the uncovered area and then cut out around that part of the pattern. Since size XL for Vest Style C will not quite fit on the 15"-wide Yukata fabric, you can add a coordinating fabric to either the center front or the side to accommodate the pattern piece.

---

# Fancy Turquoise

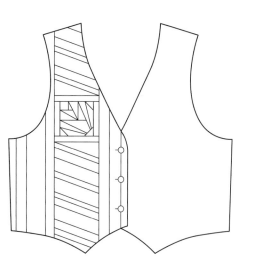

## VEST FACTS

Technique 3
Page 26

**Color photo: page 37**
**Vest Style B Option**

**Fabrics:** The large-scale print with gold accents on the left side is the main-player fabric. The strip piecing is done in matching medium blues and greens. A solid black polished cotton forms the background of the paper-pieced block. A small-scale black-on-black print is used for the back. The gold metallic fabric in the paper-pieced block picks up the gold accents in the large-scale print.

## Materials: 44"-wide fabrics

**Back:** ¾ yd.* small-scale black-on-black print
**Left Front:** ¾ yd.* large-scale multicolor print with metallic gold
**Foundation:** ¾ yd.* dark cotton (1 front)
**Right Front:** ⅛ yd. each of 3 medium blue and 2 medium green prints and 1 medium green solid, ⅛ yd. small black-and-blue stripe, and ⅛ yd. black polished cotton
**Paper-Pieced Block:** Small scrap of gold metallic fabric

*Vest Style B Option, size small. Refer to the chart on page 10 for other styles and sizes.

## Cutting and Piecing

*Cut additional strips as needed if you are making a larger size or a different style.*
1. Cut out the back.
2. Cut out the left front.
3. Cut out a right front foundation.
4. Paper-piece 1 Flower Block #6. Include the piece across the corner.

F6

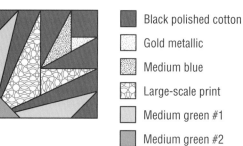

- ■ Black polished cotton
- □ Gold metallic
- ▨ Medium blue
- ▨ Large-scale print
- □ Medium green #1
- ▨ Medium green #2

5. To frame the paper-pieced block, cut 2 strips of black polished cotton, each 1" x 3½", and join to opposite sides. Cut 2 more strips, each 1" x 4½", and join to remaining sides. Remove the paper from the back of the paper-pieced block. The block should now measure 4½" x 4½".

6. From each of the blue and green prints and solid, the black-and-blue stripe, the remaining back fabric, and the remaining large-scale print, cut 1 strip, ranging from 1¼" to 1¾" wide (total of 9 strips).

7. From the remaining back fabric, cut a 3" x 6" rectangle. Cut in half diagonally as shown in the illustration and foundation-piece to the paper-pieced block.

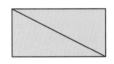

Cut 3" x 6" rectangle diagonally
corner to corner in this direction

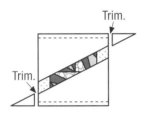

Foundation-piece triangles
to top and bottom of block.

8. Position the framed paper-pieced block on the foundation as shown in the vest plan and draw a stop-sewing line on the foundation along each vertical side. (See page 29.) Foundation-piece strips diagonally above and below the block between the stop-sewing lines. Trim the excess fabric.

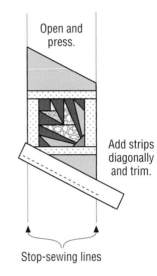

9. Once all the diagonal strips have been added, foundation-piece vertical strips to both sides until the foundation is completely covered.

Optional: Add light blue decorative stitching along diagonal seams.

10. For "Assembly and Finishing," see pages 70–74.

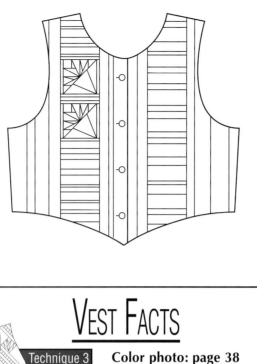

# Something Old

---

## VEST FACTS

**Technique 3
Page 26**

**Color photo: page 38
Vest Style A**

**Fabrics:** The neutral colors in the beige-taupe-and-off-white floral print used at the edge of the front is the main-player fabric for this vest. Several different off-white, beige, and taupe prints and a taupe satin make up the right and left fronts. I also included three ribbons and several laces of the same colors. A small scrap of gold metallic fabric provides the accent in the two paper-pieced Nosegay blocks. I used a small-scale taupe-and-white stripe for the back.

## Materials: 44"-wide fabrics

**Back:** ³⁄₄ yd.* small-scale taupe-and-white stripe
**Foundation:** ³⁄₄ yd.* light cotton (2 fronts)
**Right and Left Fronts:** ¹⁄₈ yd. beige-taupe-and-off-white floral print, ¹⁄₈ yd. each of 6 taupe, beige, and white prints, and ¹⁄₈ yd. taupe satin
**Paper-Pieced Blocks:** Small scrap of gold metallic fabric
**Embellishments:** 3 ribbons (2¹⁄₂", 1¹⁄₄", and 1" wide)**, 2 lace strips (¹⁄₂" and 1" wide), and lace appliqués, beads, and pearls

*Vest Style A, size small. Refer to the chart on page 10 for other styles and sizes.
**In my vest, the 1¹⁄₄"-wide ribbon runs vertically at the buttonholes—if you want to do the same thing, you will need a ribbon long enough to extend the length of your vest front.

## Cutting and Piecing

*Cut additional strips as needed if you are making a larger size or a different style.*
1. Cut out the back.
2. Cut out a right and a left front foundation.
3. Paper-piece 2 Nosegay blocks (F24). This is one of the two-section paper-pieced block designs. (See page 24.) Remember to machine baste the center seam and check for a good match before you sew the halves together permanently. Press the center seam open.

F24

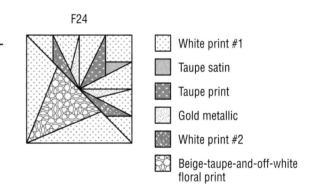

☐ White print #1
▦ Taupe satin
▨ Taupe print
░ Gold metallic
▩ White print #2
▤ Beige-taupe-and-off-white floral print

4. To frame the Nosegay blocks, cut 4 strips of taupe satin, each ¾" x 3½", and join to opposite sides on each of the 2 blocks. Cut 4 more strips, each ¾" x 4", and join to the remaining 2 sides of each block. Remove the paper from the back of the paper-pieced blocks. The blocks should measure 4" x 4". Join the 2 blocks with a 1"-wide strip of ribbon.

5. From each of the 6 taupe, beige, and white prints, the floral print and the remaining back fabric, cut 2 strips, ranging from 1" to 1¾" wide, for a total of 16 strips.

6. Center the joined paper-pieced blocks right side up on the right foundation and draw a stop-sewing line on the foundation along each vertical side. (See page 29.) Foundation-piece 4"-long horizontal strips of fabric, ribbon, and lace above and below the blocks in a random fashion, stopping at the stop-sewing lines. Precut strips to save time. Trim excess.

   Remember that you can also topstitch the ribbon to the fabric strips. (See "Ribbons and Lace" on page 31.) I created pintucking from 3 of the fabrics and cut these manipulated fabrics into 4" strips. (See "Fabric Manipulations" on page 31.)

7. Once all the horizontal strips have been added, foundation-piece vertical strips to both sides until the foundation is completely covered.

8. Mark 2 vertical stop-sewing lines on the left front, starting the same distance from the front edge as the horizontal strip piecing on the right front.

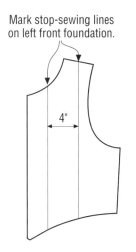

Mark stop-sewing lines on left front foundation.

4"

9. Foundation-piece the horizontal and vertical strips in the same manner as the right front, omitting the paper-pieced blocks.

   Optional: Embellish with lace appliqués, pearls, buttons, and other trinkets before joining the vest to its reversible side.

10. For "Assembly and Finishing," see pages 70–74.

# Madam Butterfly

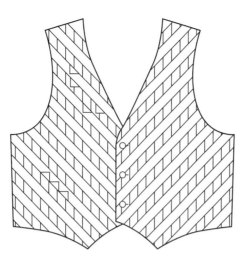

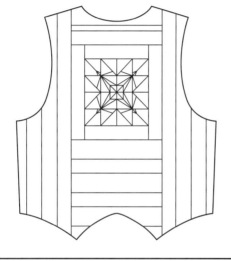

## VEST FACTS

**Technique 3
Page 26**

**Color photo: page 36
Vest Style B Option**

**Fabrics:** The main-player fabric in this vest is the metallic gold-gray-and-black floral print I used as an alternating strip on the right and left fronts. A five-fabric grouping in black, gray, and metallic gold is combined with a small-scale black-and-metallic gold print (also used on the back) in the pieced strips. Small scraps of gold metallic and gold satin accent fabrics are set against a black polished cotton in the four paper-pieced Butterfly blocks on the back. A horizontal strip of black-and-metallic gold embroidered ribbon embellishes the vest back.

## Materials: 44"-wide fabrics

**Foundation:** ¾ yd.* dark cotton (2 fronts and 1 back)

**Back:** ¾ yd.* small-scale black-and-metallic gold print

**Right and Left Fronts:** ⅛ yd. (¼ yd.**) each of 2 black prints, 1 black moiré, 1 solid metallic gray, and 1 gold lamé print (5-fabric group); and ½ yd. (¾ yd.**) medium-scale metallic gold-gray-and-black floral

**Prairie Points:** Scraps of black and gold satins and gray moiré

**Paper-Pieced Blocks:** ⅛ yd. black polished cotton, ⅛ yd. black satin for border, and scraps of gold metallic and gold satin fabrics

**Embellishment:** ⅓ yd. of 1⅛"-wide black-and-gold ribbon

*Vest Style B Option, size small. Refer to the chart on page 10 for other styles and sizes.

** Increased yardage for L and XL Vests A and B, and all sizes of Vest C.

## Cutting and Piecing

*Cut additional strips as needed if you are making a larger size or a different style.*

Cut out one right front, one left front, and one back foundation.

### FRONTS

1. From the 5-fabric group and the back fabric, cut the following:

   Select 2 fabrics. From each fabric, cut 2 strips, each 1¾" wide (total of 4 strips).

   Select 2 other fabrics. From each, cut 2 strips, each 1½" wide (total of 4 strips).

   From each of the last 2 fabrics, cut 2 strips, each 1¼" wide (total of 4 strips).

2. Make 2 strip sets as shown and press. (Be careful of the delicate fabrics when pressing. Lower the heat setting and use a pressing cloth.)

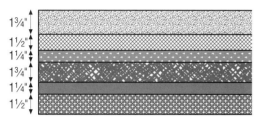

Make 2 sets.

3. To cut strips for the left front only, cut off the corner at a 45° angle as shown. Cut 11 pieced strips, each 1½" wide, parallel to the first cut. (See "Making Pieced Strips" on pages 14–16.)

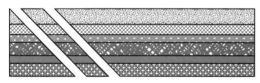

Left Front

4. From the main-player fabric, cut 6 strips, each 1½" x 42" (3 for each front).

5. Join 2 of the pieced strips end to end to form a strip long enough to cover the longest diagonal portion of the left front. Pin in place. Foundation-piece a main-player strip to each long side. Continue to alternate pieced strips with main-player strips, joining pieced strips as needed. Don't try to match up seams in alternating pieced rows. Watch those angles! Insert a few prairie points between seams.

6. To make the right front, cut off the corner of the remaining strip-pieced unit at a 45° angle as shown. Cut 11 strips, each 1½" wide, parallel to the first cut.

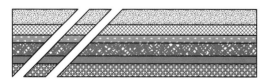

Right Front

7. Complete the right front in the same manner as the left, piecing strips diagonally in the opposite direction.

## BACK

1. Paper-piece 4 Butterfly blocks (P13). This is one of the two-section paper-pieced block designs. (See page 24.) Since one side is the mirror image of the other, it is easiest to piece both sides simultaneously. Machine baste the center seam and check for a good match before sewing the halves together permanently. Join the completed blocks as shown.

P13

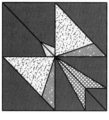 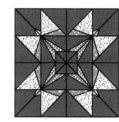

Make 4.          Join 4 Butterfly blocks.

Black polished cotton
Gold metallic
Gold metallic lamé print
Gold satin
Metallic gold-gray-and-black floral print

2. To frame the joined blocks with black satin, cut 2 strips, each 1¾" x 6½", and sew to the top and bottom. Cut 2 more strips, each 1¾" x 9", and sew to each side. Remove the paper from the back of the paper-pieced blocks.

3. Center the framed block on the back foundation, slightly above midback. Draw a vertical stop-sewing line on the foundation along each side, even with the edge of the frame. (See page 29.)

4. From the black-and-metallic gold back fabric, cut 3 strips, each 2¼" wide, and 3 strips, each 1¾" wide. Beginning with a 2¼" strip, foundation-piece horizontal strips to the bottom of the center block between the stop-sewing lines, alternating the 2 widths. Precut strips 9" long to save time. Continue above the block in the same manner, starting with a 1¾" strip. Topstitch a decorative black-and-gold ribbon as the second strip above the center block. (See "Ribbons and Lace" on page 31.) Trim excess fabric.

5. Once all the horizontal strips have been added, begin foundation-piecing vertical strips to both sides of the center block, starting with a 1¾" strip and alternating the 2 widths until the foundation is completely covered.

6. For "Assembly and Finishing," see pages 70–74.

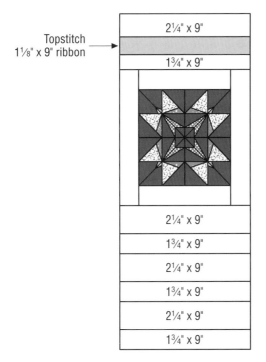

Topstitch
1⅛" x 9" ribbon

2¼" x 9"

1¾" x 9"

2¼" x 9"

1¾" x 9"

2¼" x 9"

1¾" x 9"

2¼" x 9"

1¾" x 9"

## Cutting and Piecing

*Cut additional strips as needed if you are making a larger size or a different style.*

1. Cut out the back.
2. Cut out a right and a left front foundation.
3. Paper-piece one 3" Heart and Flower block.

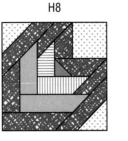

H8

- ☐ Light blue satin pindot
- ▨ Darker blue print
- ▥ Light blue silk
- ‖ White-and-silver stripe
- ▢ Light blue satin

4. From each of the 5 (6 or 7) blue prints, the remaining back fabric, and the larger-scale leaf print, cut 2 strips, each 1½" wide, for a total of 14 (16 or 18) strips.
5. Join strips, Log Cabin fashion, around all 4 sides of the paper-pieced block and remove the paper. (See page 28.)
6. Make several prairie points out of the silk and satin fabrics used in the paper-pieced block.
7. Position the block on the left front foundation and continue to add Log Cabin strips until the entire foundation is covered. Add prairie points in the first seams surrounding the block.
8. Complete the right front by foundation-piecing vertical strips of all fabrics except the back fabric. Topstitch 1 strip of silver satin ribbon, using straight pins to hold it in place. Add prairie points randomly.

Optional: Stitch tiny seed pearls at the tip of each prairie point and along the top edge of the paper-pieced flower.

9. For "Assembly and Finishing," see pages 70–74.

## VEST FACTS

| Technique 3 Page 26 | Color photo: page 34 Vest Style A |

**Fabrics:** I started with a blue-and-silver leaf fabric and used it in the strip piecing on both vest fronts. I added five subtle blue-and-white prints in very similar values, with a slightly darker blue print on the back. Scraps of light blue satin, light blue pindot satin, light blue silk, and a white-and-silver stripe are used in the paper-pieced Heart and Flower block and as prairie-point accents. One strip of silver satin ribbon shimmers on the right front.

## Materials: 44"-wide fabrics

**Back:** ¾ yd.* medium-scale darker blue print
**Foundation:** ¾ yd.* light cotton (2 fronts)
**Right and Left Fronts:** ⅛ yd. each of 5 (6 or 7**) subtle blue-and-white prints, ⅛ yd. larger-scale blue-and-silver leaf print, and ¾ yd.* 1¼"-wide silver satin ribbon
**Paper-Pieced Blocks and Prairie Points:** Small scraps of light blue satins and silks and a white-and-metallic silver stripe
**Embellishment:** Seed pearls

   *Vest Style A, size small. Refer to the chart on page 10 for other styles and sizes.

   **Use 6 fabrics for Vest A and B, sizes M to XL. Use 7 fabrics for all sizes of Vest C.

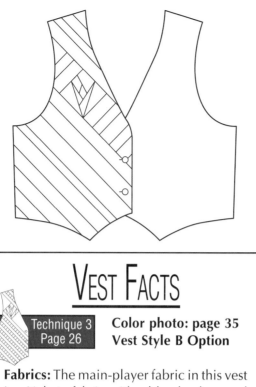

## VEST FACTS

| Technique 3 Page 26 | **Color photo: page 35**<br>**Vest Style B Option** |
|---|---|

**Fabrics:** The main-player fabric in this vest is a Yukata fabric with a blue background and purple and coral flowers. The strip piecing is done in matching blues and purples. An almost-black navy and a light coral are the accent colors. Polished cotton fabrics provide a different texture. The back is a medium-scale blue-and-black print.

## Materials: 44"-wide fabrics

**Back:** ¾ yd.* medium-scale blue-and-black print
**Left Front:** ¾ yd.* Yukata print
**Foundation:** ¾ yd.* dark cotton (1 front)
**Right Front:** Scraps (at least 1" wide) of a variety of solids and prints in deep dark blue, blue, coral, and purple (approximately ½ yd. total)**
**Paper-Pieced Block:** Large scrap of blue polished cotton for the background

*Vest Style B Option, size small. Refer to the chart on page 10 for other styles and sizes.

**Scraps must be long enough to fit diagonally across the vest front.

## Cutting and Piecing

*Cut additional strips as needed if you are making a larger size or a different style.*

1. Cut out the back.
2. Cut out the left front.
3. Cut out a right front foundation.
4. Paper-piece 1 Flower Block #7.

F7

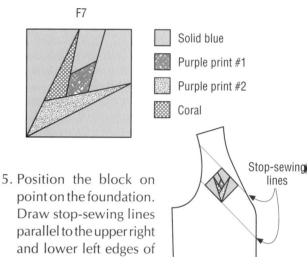

| | Solid blue |
| | Purple print #1 |
| | Purple print #2 |
| | Coral |

5. Position the block on point on the foundation. Draw stop-sewing lines parallel to the upper right and lower left edges of the block as shown.

6. From the scraps and the remaining back fabric, cut strips ranging from 1" to 1¾" wide.

7. With the paper still on, foundation-piece 3½"-long strips to the upper left and lower right of the paper-pieced block, stopping at the stop-sewing lines. Remove the thin strips of paper from the seam allowances of the paper-pieced block. Continue to add strips between the stop-sewing lines. Trim excess fabric.

8. Once you have added short strips all the way out to the edges of the pattern piece, foundation-piece long strips across the first group. Remove the paper from the seam allowances. Insert 2 prairie points along the dark strip above the paper-pieced strip. Continue to foundation-piece strips diagonally until the foundation is covered. Watch those angles!

9. Carefully slit the foundation behind the paper-pieced block and remove the paper. (See page 27.) (This is one of those times when foundation piecing with the paper intact seems easier.)

10. For "Assembly and Finishing," see pages 70–74.

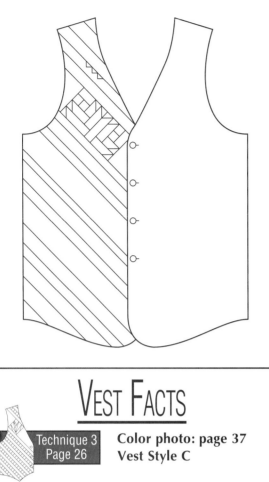

*Vest Style C, size medium. Refer to the chart on page 10 for other styles and sizes.

## Cutting and Piecing

*Cut additional strips as needed if you are making a larger size or a different style.*

1. Cut out the back.
2. Cut out the left front.
3. Cut out a right front foundation.
4. From the remaining back fabric, the dark blue and navy blue polished cottons, and the 6 medium to dark blue prints, cut 1 strip each in random widths ranging from 1½" to 2½".
5. Paper-piece 2 Flower Block #3.

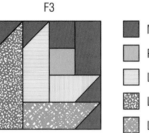

F3

- Navy polished cotton
- Pink scrap
- Light blue scrap #1
- Light blue scrap #2
- Light blue scrap #3

6. Join the paper-pieced blocks together and position on the right front foundation as shown in the vest plan. Measure the length needed to cover the foundation on either side. Watch those angles! Remove the blocks from the foundation. Cut and add 3½"-wide strips of the back fabric to the upper left side and the lower right side of the joined blocks. (See page 26.)
7. Choose 2 fabric strips from those cut in step 4. Position the pieced strip on the foundation to determine the necessary length of the fabric strips. Remember to watch those angles! Remove the pieced strip from the foundation and sew a fabric strip to each long side. Remove the paper and pin the paper-pieced strip in position on the foundation.
8. Foundation-piece diagonal strips above and below the paper-pieced unit, concentrating the medium value fabrics in the upper portion and the darker value fabrics in the lower portion. Insert 3 prairie points in one of the strips above the paper-pieced unit.
9. For "Assembly and Finishing," see pages 70–74.

# VEST FACTS

**Technique 3**
**Page 26**

**Color photo: page 37**
**Vest Style C**

**Fabrics:** The main-player fabric in this vest is a Yukata fabric with light blue flowers and pink centers on a dark blue background. The right front patchwork consists of a group of six dark blue-and-black prints and medium blue fabrics. Navy blue and dark blue polished cotton fabrics are also included. Scraps of pink fabric and three lighter blue fabrics are used in the paper-pieced flower blocks set against the navy blue polished cotton. The back is a subtle blue-and-black medium-scale print.

## Materials: 44"- wide fabrics

**Back:** 1 yd.* medium-scale blue and black print
**Left Front:** 1 yd.* Yukata floral print
**Foundation:** 1 yd.* dark cotton (1 front)
**Right Front:** ⅛ yd. each of 6 dark blue-and-black prints and medium blue fabrics; ⅛ yd. each of a dark blue and navy blue polished cotton
**Paper-Pieced Blocks:** Small scraps of pink and 3 lighter blue fabrics

# Hearts and Flowers

## Vest Facts

**Technique 3 Page 26** | **Color photo: page 38 Vest Style A**

**Fabrics:** The main-player fabric is the large-scale pastel floral on the left side. Eight light green fabrics similar in color to the floral's background round out the fabric choices. A darker green-pink-and-metallic gold stripe serves as an accent fabric. Scraps of even darker green moiré, pink satin, and gold metallic are used in the paper-pieced Heart and Flower blocks on the front and back. A small print with pink and green flowers creates delicate hearts in the paper-pieced blocks, providing contrast against the light green background.

## Materials: 44"-wide fabrics

**Left Front:** 3/4 yd.* large-scale pastel floral
**Foundation:** 3/4 yd.* light cotton (1 front and 1 back)
**Back and Right Front:** 1/4 yd. lightest light green, 1/8 yd. each of 7 additional light greens, and 1/8 yd. darker green-pink-and-gold stripe
**Paper-Pieced Blocks:** 1/8 yd. pink and green print on white background and scraps of green moiré, pink satin, and gold metallic
**Embellishments:** 2 small lace heart appliqués, small pink glass beads, and gold metallic machine-embroidery thread

*Vest Style A, size small. Refer to the chart on page 10 for Vest Style B and B option and for other sizes. Yardage is not included to make Vest Style C, since this back design is not suggested for Vest Style C.

## Cutting and Piecing

*Cut additional strips as needed if you are making a larger size or a different style.*

1. Cut out the left front.
2. Cut out a back and a right front foundation.
3. Paper-piece 1 each of the 3" and 6" Heart and Flower blocks.

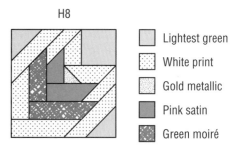

H8

- ▨ Lightest green
- ▦ White print
- ▨ Gold metallic
- ▨ Pink satin
- ▨ Green moiré

4. Position the 3" block on the right front foundation as shown in the vest plan. Measure the approximate length needed to cover the foundation on either side. Remove the block from the foundation. From the lightest green fabric, cut 2 strips, each 3 1/2" wide and long enough to cover the foundation. Sew strips to the upper left and lower right edges of the block.

5. Position the paper-pieced strip on the right front foundation again and measure the length needed for the strips above and below. Cut 1¼"-wide strips of the lightest green fabric to length. Remove the paper-pieced strip from the foundation, add green strips, and remove the paper from the back of the paper-pieced blocks. Pin the paper-pieced strip in place on the right foundation.

6. From each of the 7 remaining green fabrics and the large-scale pastel floral, cut 2 strips, ranging from 1¼" to 1¾" wide. Cut 1 strip, 1¼" wide, from the striped accent fabric.

7. Foundation-piece these strips in a random fashion diagonally above and below the paper-pieced strip until the foundation is covered. Watch those angles! Trim excess fabric. Position the 2 lace heart appliqués to the right and left of the paper-pieced heart and machine stitch in place. Embellish the lace hearts with small pink glass beads.

8. From the pastel floral, cut 2 squares, each 5⅛" x 5⅛", and cut each square once diagonally. Sew a triangle to each of the 4 sides of the 6" paper-pieced block. (See Tip on page 26.) Remove the paper from the back of the paper-pieced block.

9. To find the center of the back foundation, press it in half vertically and then horizontally at the point where the armholes begin to curve out toward the sides. Unfold. Using these press lines as a guide, center the framed 6" paper-pieced block on the back foundation and pin in place. Draw horizontal stop-sewing lines across the foundation even with the top and bottom edges of the block. (See page 29.)

10. Foundation-piece vertical strips in a random fashion to the right and left of the block until the area is covered. Precut strips to save time. Trim excess fabric.

11. Foundation-piece horizontal strips above and below until the foundation is completely covered.

   **Optional:** Embellish with metallic machine-embroidery thread and a variety of decorative stitches along several seam lines and in the middle of strips.

---

# TIP

Use a machine topstitch needle when using the metallic thread. Test the decorative stitch and thread before using them on your vest.

---

12. This vest has ruffled shoulder accents made of 2 different fabrics. One side matches this vest and the other side matches the reverse vest. For this vest side, cut 2 strips, each 2½" x 15½", from the lightest green fabric. (See "Shoulder Accents" on page 32.)

13. For "Assembly and Finishing," see pages 70–74.

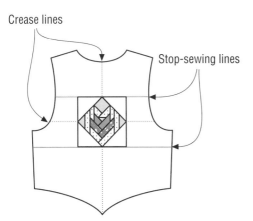

Crease lines

Stop-sewing lines

Once you have completed two fronts and a back for each vest side, it is time to sew the pieces together. Use the walking foot attachment to assemble the vest sides.

1. Cut interfacing pieces from fusible interfacing.
2. Fuse interfacing pieces to the wrong side of one vest side.
3. Place the 2 fronts of one vest side on the back, right sides together, and pin the shoulder seams.
4. Sew with a ⅜"-wide seam allowance and press the seams open. Repeat with other vest side.

> Note: If you are using a commercial pattern that has a ⅝"-wide seam allowance, sew as directed and trim the seam allowances to ⅜".

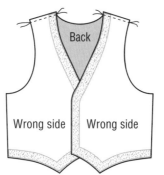

Now is the time to add ruffled or pleated shoulder accents and button loops. (See "Shoulder Accents" on page 32 and "Buttons and Closures" on pages 72–73.)

*To join the two sides of a reversible vest:*
1. Lay one vest side on top of the other side, right sides together. Pin the armholes and the bottom edge of the back. Pin the bottom edge of the front, continuing up around the center front and neck edges, matching all seams. *Do not pin the side openings.*

2. Stitch the two sides together as illustrated, using a ⅜"-wide seam allowance. Do not stitch the sides of the fronts or back.

Do not stitch the side seams
in the front or the back!

3. Clip all curves around the neck and armholes. Cut across points ¼" from the stitching to reduce bulk. Clip any inside angles.

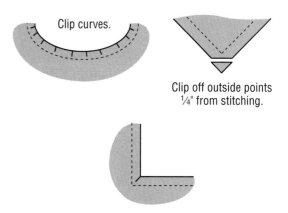

Clip curves.

Clip off outside points
¼" from stitching.

Clip inside angles.

4. Once the two vests have been joined, trimmed, and clipped, reach in from one of the back side openings to turn the vest right side out. Pull each front out the side opening as shown.

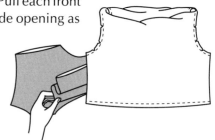

5. Use a blunt tool to push out points and to run along the seams to push out the edges. The Stuff-It II™ tool described in the supplies list works well for this task.

6. Steam press along the seams.

Caution: If you are using heat-sensitive synthetic fabrics in your vest, use a pressing cloth and lower the iron temperature.

# Elastic

Before you stitch the side seams, you have still another option available! You can add a section of elastic to the lower center back to create the illusion of a more fitted vest back.

1. Find the center back at the waistline. Lightly mark a horizontal line about 5" long. Mark another horizontal line 1" above the first line.

2. Stitch along the parallel lines, through both vest backs. Use one color of thread on the top and another color of thread in the bobbin to match the other vest side if necessary.

3. Feed ¾"-wide elastic between the 2 stitching lines and stitch across one end. Pull the elastic enough to gather up the fabric slightly and stitch the other end. Cut the elastic off about ½" from the end stitching lines.

Feed elastic between
2 lines of stitching.

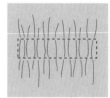

Close-up of gathered back strip

# Side Seams

1. Pin the front to the back at the sides between the armhole seam and bottom seam, right sides together. If one of the sides has been foundation-pieced, start with it, because it is harder to hand sew foundation piecing. Follow the illustration below for pinning the seam allowances at the armhole, and continue pinning to the hem.

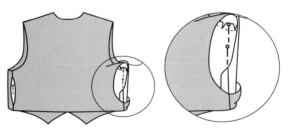

Place seam allowances in opposite directions
so they will "lock." (Side edges are shown offset
so you can see position of seam allowances.)

2. Try the vest on to check for a good fit. Adjust the side seams if necessary.

3. Sew the side seams from the bottom up, backstitching at the beginning and end. Press the seam allowances toward the back of the vest.

4. Lay the pieced section (if any) of the unsewn vest flat and overlap the single fabric side, turning under ⅜". Press and blindstitch.

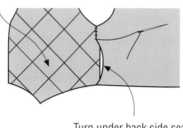

Lay pieced front flat.

Turn under back side seam ⅜" for hand sewing.

# Vest Style C— Side Vent Option

To make Vest Style C with side vents, stitch the layered vests as shown. Backstitch at the notches.

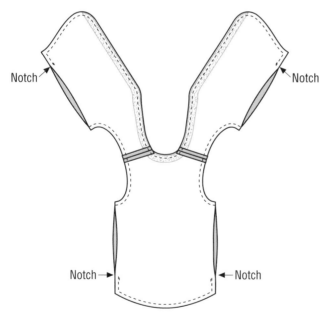

Notch

Notch

Notch →

← Notch

Clip the curves and turn the vest out to the right side. Pin the side seam of one vest side, right sides together, so that the remainder of this side seam can be sewn to the armhole. Stitch.

Repeat with the other side seam of the other vest side. Finish in the same manner as previously described.

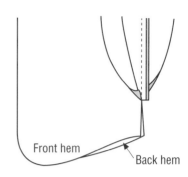

Front hem

Back hem

# Buttons and Closures

Buttons are an opportunity for creativity as well. I once used buttons that looked like thimbles and a 1" portion of a ruler on a strip-pieced vest, which I thought was very appropriate. The buttons you choose can be the perfect finishing touch to your original fashion vest.

You have several options when it comes to closing your reversible vest. Women's clothing routinely closes right over left. The buttons are on the left side, and the buttonholes or loops are on the right side. For both sides of the reversible vest to close this way, you need to make two sets of buttonholes.

To do this and still conceal the other buttonhole when the vest is buttoned, place the buttons and buttonholes as shown. Place the buttonholes close to the edge and use small buttons and short buttonholes. When sewing the buttons on, make sure the thread does not go all the way through to the other side of the vest. When the vest is buttoned, the extra buttonholes on the edge are hidden, and both vests button right over left.

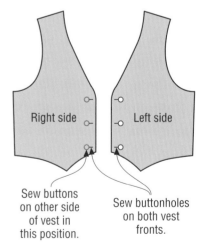

Right side

Left side

Sew buttons on other side of vest in this position.

Sew buttonholes on both vest fronts.

Another option is to use only one set of buttonholes or loops for both vest sides and button right over left on one side and left over right on the other side. I have used this option often and no one has ever brought to my attention that the vest that buttons left over right is unconventional for the female population. People are used to seeing clothing close in both directions, and the distinction is not something most people notice. Consider it a new fashion trend!

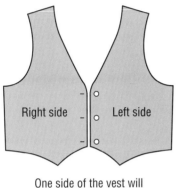

One side of the vest will
button right over left.

The reverse side of the vest
will button left over right.

*To add buttons:*
1. Choose 2 sets of shank-style buttons, all the same size.
2. Sew the buttonholes (or loops) on the right front of one of the patchwork vest sides.

# TIP

You can use two different colors of thread to make the buttonholes. The color on the top can match the side of the vest facing up and the color in the bobbin can match the vest underneath.

3. On the other front, sew a button on one side of the vest. Bring the needle through to the reverse side of the vest and slip the other button on the needle; sew it back to back with the first button.

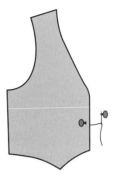

# TIP

To cut the opening in machine-made buttonholes, I use a flat-edge X-acto® knife rather than scissors. The knife makes a clean cut as you press down, and you don't risk snipping too far.

Still another option is to make fabric loops and pin them along the center front seam before joining the two sides of the vest. The seam secures the loops into position. With this option, the vest buttons in two directions as described above.

*To make fabric loops:*
1. Cut a narrow bias strip (about 1" wide and 10" long for 3 loops).
2. Fold the strip lengthwise, right sides together, and sew ¼" from the raw edges. Trim the seam allowances close to the stitching.

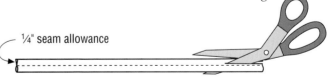

¼" seam allowance

Fold

3. Turn the bias strip right side out and press. This is not an easy task with such a thin piece of fabric. Some wonderful tools, such as the Miniturn™, are available to help you do this. (See Resource List on page 88.)

4. Decide how long each loop needs to be to fit over the buttons you are using and add ¾" for seam allowances. I use 3" lengths for most buttons. Cut 3 lengths and fold the lengths as shown. Pin them on the right side of the vest front that you want to go right over left as shown, and machine baste in place ⅛" from the edge.

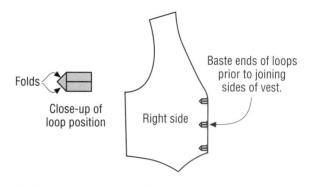

Folds

Close-up of loop position

Right side

Baste ends of loops prior to joining sides of vest.

5. Try on the vest to determine button placement. Buttons for loops are usually sewn a little farther from the front edge than regular buttons.

# Block Designs

## Paper-Pieced Block Designs

The designs in this book are grouped by categories. Eight of the designs are also included in my book *Easy Machine Paper Piecing* in a 4" size. The remaining 29 designs are new 3" blocks created specifically for the vests in this book.

Rather than name each of the block designs as is normally the case in patchwork, I have assigned letters and numbers that continue from my other book. For example, Flower blocks F1 through F14 can be found in *Easy Machine Paper Piecing*; F15 through F26 are new blocks in this book.

### 3" Block Designs

The lines on the block design represent the sewing lines, and the numbers represent the piecing sequence. Using paper piecing to make blocks is quick; however, a block with five pieces is still faster to piece than a block with seventeen pieces.

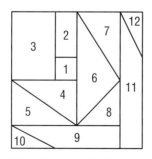

3" Block Design (stitching side)

The 3" block design represents the wrong side of the block. This is of no consequence for symmetrical blocks with symmetrical fabric placement. However, asymmetrical blocks or asymmetrical fabric placement will result in the reverse pattern appearing on the finished side.

The dotted lines in some block designs signal the opportunity to create a variation of the design by including or deleting those particular seam lines.

### Block-Front Drawings

These small drawings show how the finished blocks will appear from the fabric side. They can be photocopied and used for design purposes. Use colored pencils to try different color schemes. Always use the block-front drawings to make your design and color selection and note your choices on the unmarked side of the corresponding 3" block designs.

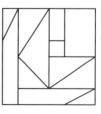

Block-Front Drawing

# FLOWERS

### F1

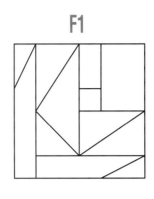

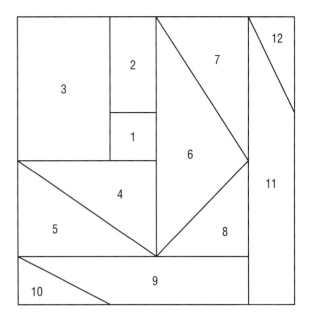

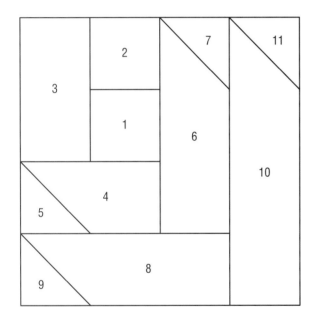

### F3

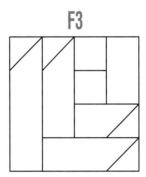

### F6

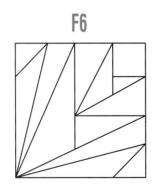

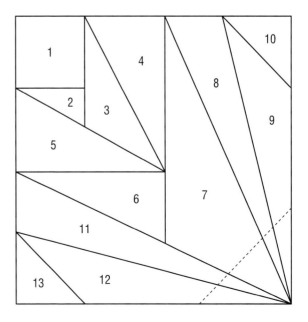

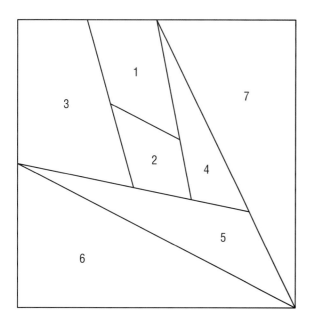

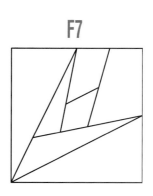
**F7**

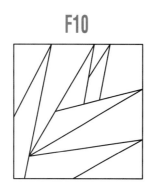
**F10**

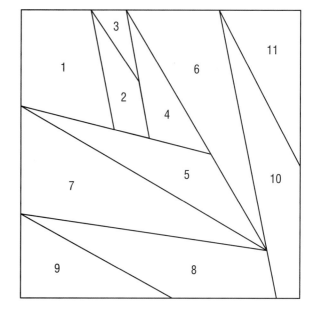

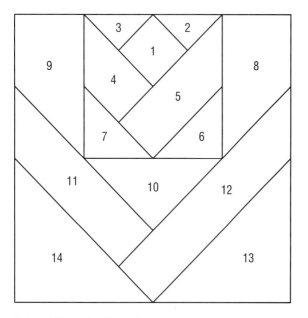

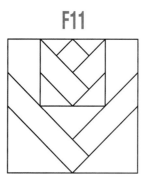
**F11**

**F15**

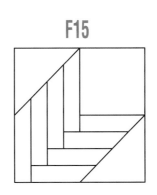

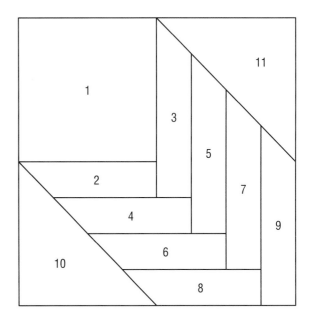

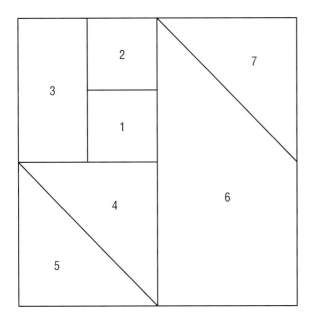

**F16**

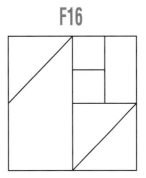

**F17**

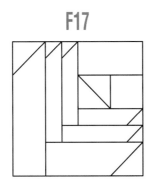

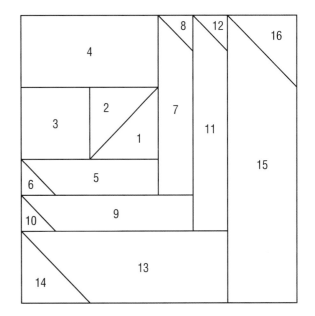

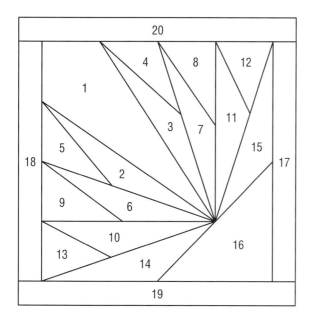

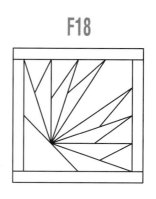

**F18**

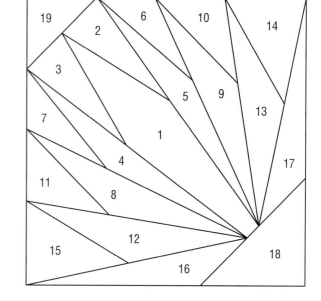

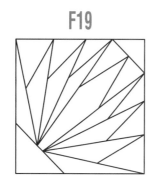

**F19**

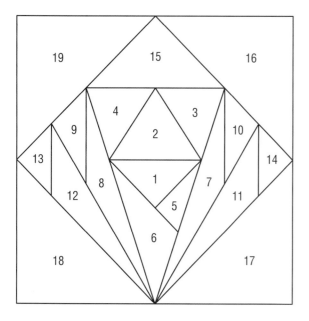

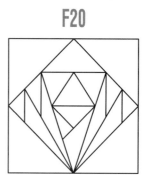

**F20**

**F21**

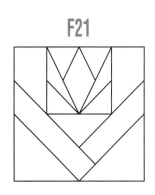

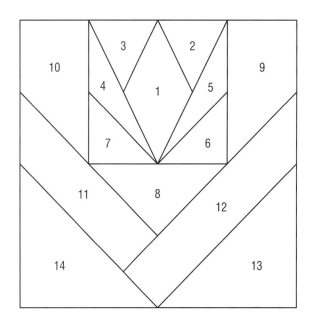

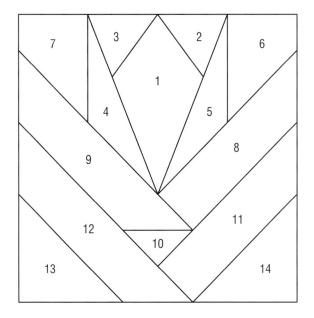

**F22**

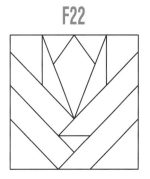

**F23**

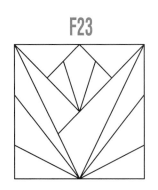

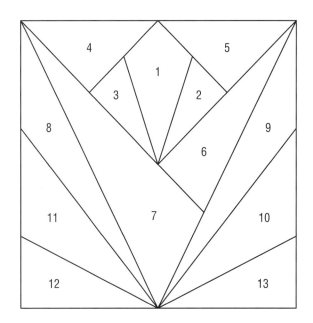

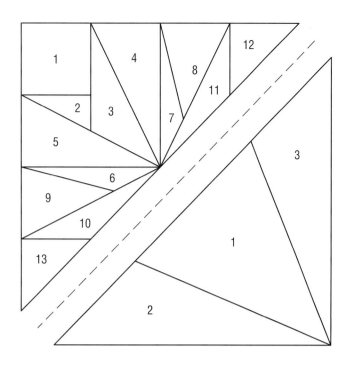

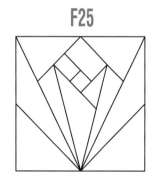

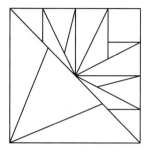

**F24**

**F25**

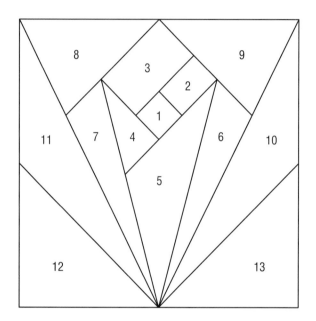

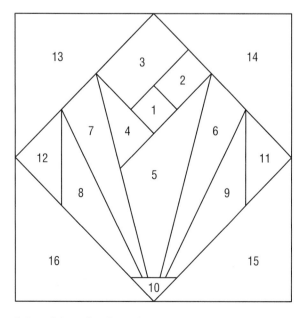

**F26**

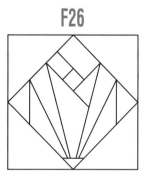

80 Block Designs

# HEARTS

## H8

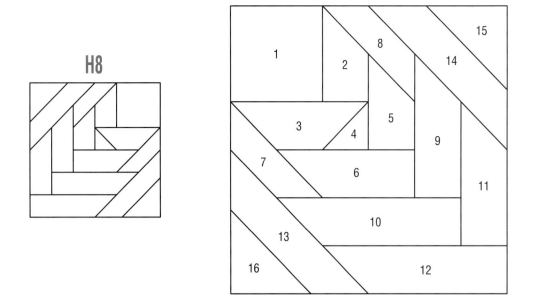

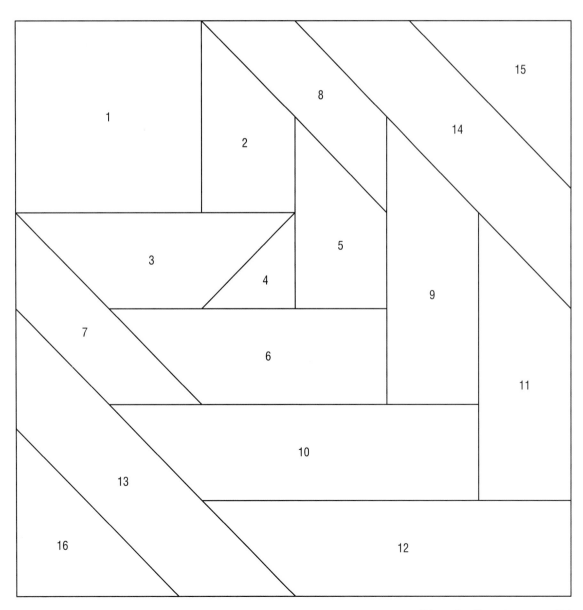

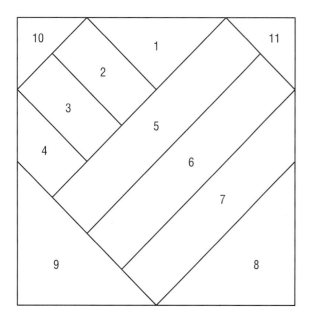

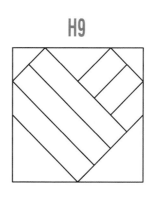

**H9**

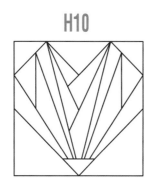

**H10**

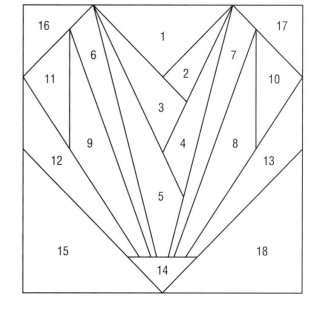

**PICTURES**

**P10**

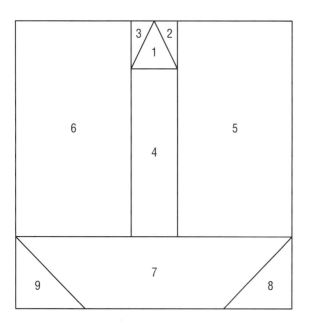

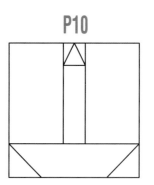

82 Block Designs

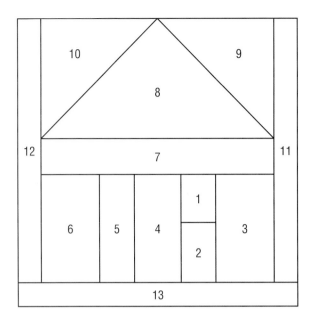

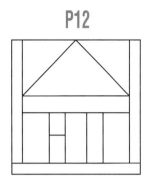

## P12

## P13

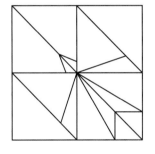

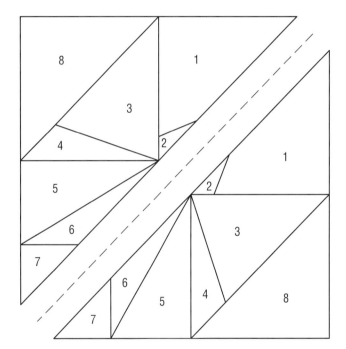

## TREE

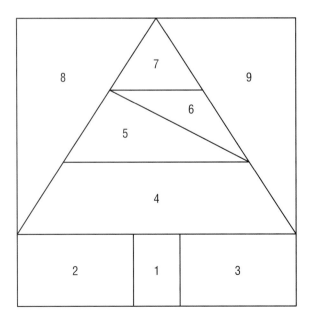

## T8

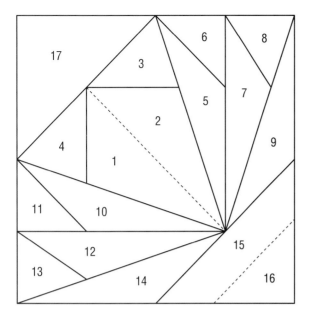

**G5**

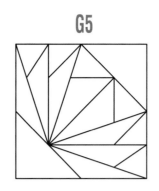

**G19**

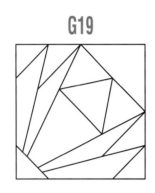

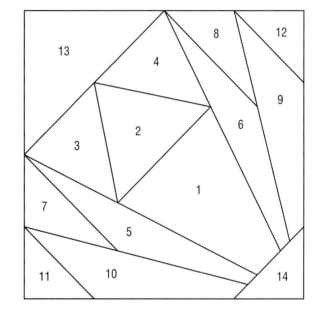

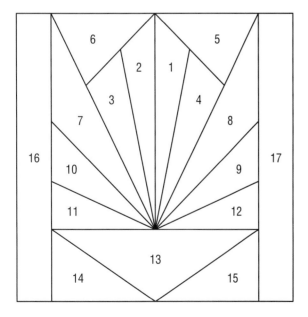

**G20**

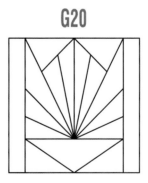

## G21

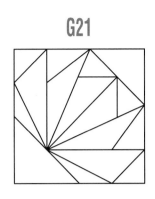

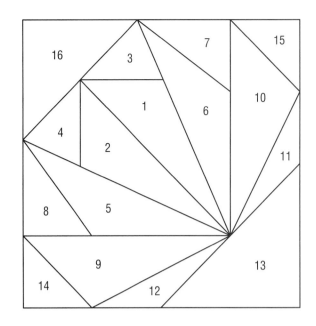

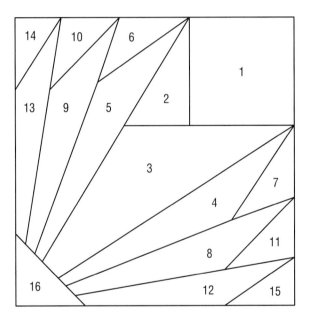

## G22

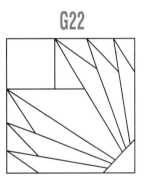

## G23

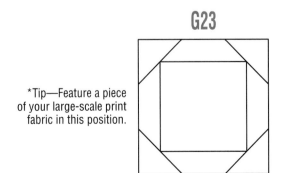

*Tip—Feature a piece of your large-scale print fabric in this position.

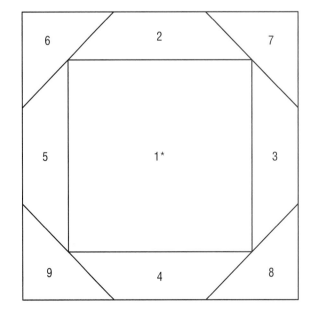

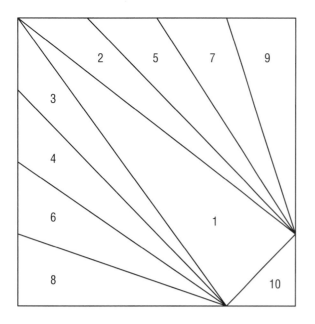

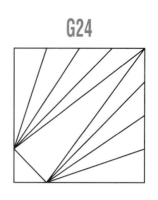
G24

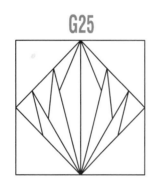
G25

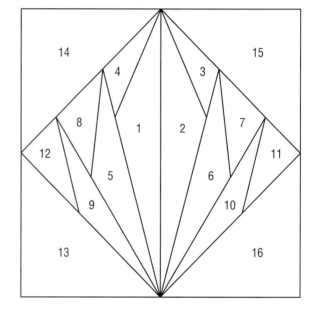

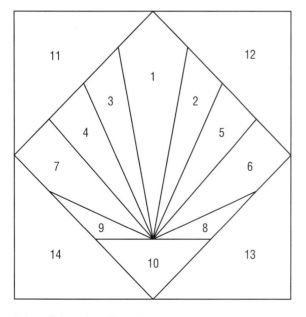

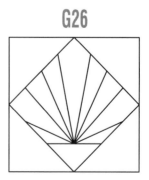
G26

# BASKETS

## B9

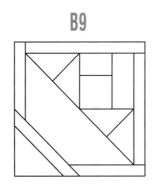

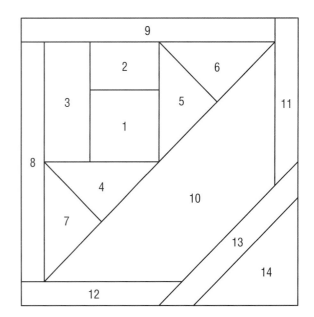

## B10

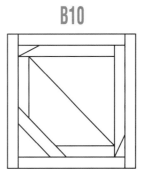

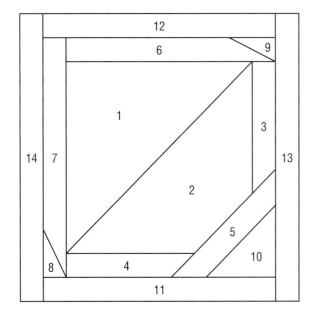

## B11

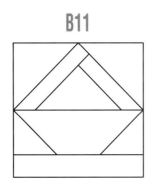

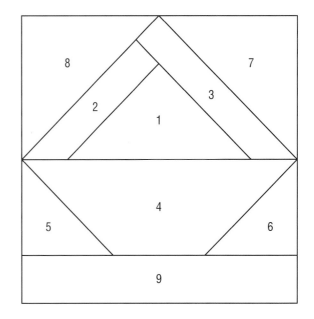

# Resource List

## The following list of suppliers and manufacturers can be contacted regarding products suggested in this book:

**Hera™ Marker**
Clover Needlecraft, Inc.
1007 E. Dominguez St., Suite "L"
Carson, California 90746

**Ruby Beholder™**
That Patchwork Place
P.O. Box 118
Bothell, Washington 98041-0118

**Miniturn™**
The Crowning Touch, Inc.
2410 Glory C Road
Medford, Oregon 97501

**Stuff-It II™**
Prairie Farm Designs
945 Range Road
Littleton, Colorado 80120

**Vendors of Japanese Yukata Fabrics**
Quilter's Express To Japan
80 East 11th Street, Suite #623
New York, New York 10003

Kasuri Dyeworks
1959 Shattuck Avenue
Berkeley, California 94704

Dolan Enterprises
P.O. Box 267
Yarmouth, Maine 04096-0267

---

## ABOUT THE AUTHOR

Carol Doak is an award-winning quiltmaker, author, and teacher. She has made over 150 quilts since taking her first quiltmaking class in Worthington, Ohio, in 1979. Carol began teaching quiltmaking almost immediately and currently travels nationally and internationally to share her quiltmaking "Tricks of the Trade." She writes a regular column of the same title for *Quick and Easy Quilting* magazine. Her lighthearted approach and ability to teach have earned her high marks and positive comments from workshop participants.

Carol's Blue Ribbon quilts have been presented in several books, such as *Great American Quilts 1990* and *The Quilt Encyclopedia.* She has been featured in several national quilt magazines, and her quilts have appeared on the cover of *Quilter's Newsletter Magazine, Quilt World,* and *Quilting Today.*

Carol's first book, *Quiltmaker's Guide: Basics & Beyond*, was published in 1992. Her second and third books, *Country Medallion Sampler* and *Easy* *Machine Paper Piecing* (both from That Patchwork Place) were published in 1993. With her easy and inspiring teaching style, Carol sees her writing as a means to reach more quiltmakers.

Carol lives with her family in Windham, New Hampshire, where the long, cold winters offer her many opportunities to cozy under quilts in progress.